Cambridge School Classics Project

War with Troy: The Story of Achilles

Teacher's Guide

Grant Bage, Jennie Dunn and Bob Lister

PUBLISHED BY THE CAMBRIDGE SCHOOL CLASSICS PROJECT
Faculty of Education, University of Cambridge,
11 West Road, Cambridge CB3 9DP, UK
http://www.CambridgeSCP.com

First published 2003

Guide and CDs printed in the United Kingdom
by Cambridge Printers, 1 Mercers Row, Cambridge CB5 8HY
and Birnam CD, Birnam
Typesetting by Gary Reynolds, Cambridge

A catalogue record for this guide is obtainable from the British Library

ISBN 0 – 9542794 – 2 – 5

Illustrations by Nick Ellis, Cambridge

Front cover: warrior based on Peloponnesian bronze figure, early seventh century
BC, Olympia Museum

ACKNOWLEDGEMENTS
For help in preparing and developing *War with Troy: The Story of Achilles* and the Teacher's Guide, we would
like to express our thanks to Ken Bingham, Les Chappell, Anne Fitzpatrick, Debbie James, Liz Lloyd, Marcus
Lodwick, Hugh Lupton, Daniel Morden, Stuart Purnell, Panos Seranis, Chloe Shannon, Sheila Skilbeck, Clare
Yerbury, and staff and pupils at:
Barking and Dagenham LEA
Norwich Road Primary School, Thetford
Redcastle Furze Primary School, Thetford
St. Joseph's Catholic Primary School, Dagenham
Thetford Education Action Zone
William Ford Junior School, Dagenham

CONTENTS

CD contents

PART 1: THE TROJAN WAR & THE CURRICULUM

PART 2: TEACHING NOTES

PART 3: TEACHING RESOURCES

THE TROJAN WAR
& THE CURRICULUM

Using the Teacher's Guide

Quick start

- To find out about how *War with Troy* was developed from Homer's *Iliad*, go to pages 7-10

- To read how *War with Troy* fits into the primary curriculum, go to pages 11-12

- To read episode-by-episode teaching notes, go to pages 18-41

- To read transcripts of each episode, go to pages 44-85

- To see visual materials to support *War with Troy* in the classroom, go to pages 87-118

The aims of the Teacher's Guide are:

- to explain why the story of Troy is so important and how it fits into the primary school curriculum (Part 1)

- to provide guidance on how to teach the story episode by episode, suggesting key questions to ask and learning objectives for literacy, and Personal Social and Health Education (PSHE) and citizenship (Part 2)

- to provide classroom resources to accompany the CDs, including a full transcript and 15 photocopiable illustrations (Part 3)

The telling of *War with Troy: The Story of Achilles* (hereafter *War with Troy*) has been created to provide a rich listening experience. It can be enjoyed by children aged nine to fourteen years with no advance preparation by the teacher. This is because the story is explained as it is told. It is not therefore *essential* to work through this guide before listening. Yet the written and visual materials in the following pages can help listeners to a richer and deeper enjoyment of the story; and enable teachers to plan for a range of important learning outcomes.

This guide has been written particularly for use with children aged nine to eleven (English school Years 5/6), with special emphasis on literacy, PSHE and citizenship. For instance, in Part 2 of the guide, many of the educational objectives are drawn from the English National Literacy Strategy document, *Framework for teaching* (DFEE 1998, hereafter NLS). Where teaching suggestions link directly to this document, you will find specific references with a brief description (e.g. NLS 6:2:1, narrative structure). Links are also made to the National Curriculum Guidelines for Key Stage 2 PSHE and citizenship (hereafter NC Guidelines), and the QCA scheme of work (QCA 1999, hereafter QCA SoW).

This *Teacher's Guide* provides initial ideas for approaching *War with Troy* rather than a definitive list. The imaginative scope and depth of the story means that it can help meet many educational objectives in areas other than Literacy or PSHE and citizenship. As you become increasingly familiar with the story, please explore such possibilities for yourselves.

Please note that further materials and resources can be found at
www.CambridgeSCP.com/myths.

WHY THIS STORY?

Why should modern teachers – or children – be interested in a three thousand year old story, from the other side of Europe?

The first reason is that this story "is the best one in the world – no question. I have told it myself dozens of times; I've listened to it, been thrilled and uplifted and terrified and moved and inspired by it for most of my lifetime." These are the words of Philip Pullman, not only an internationally acclaimed children's author, but also a teacher.

The second reason is also simple. Experience has shown us that this version of Homer's *Iliad* 'works'. *War with Troy* has been trialled in many classrooms with different children by practising teachers, researchers and storytellers. Children seem to love listening to it, and learning from it. The reading, writing, speaking and listening teaching suggestions in this guide also derive from classroom trials. These suggestions have been designed by experienced teachers, with the English National Literacy Strategy (NLS) as a particular focus.

The third reason is that *War with Troy* has been developed in a unique way: it is an oral production. The story is performed by two of Britain's leading storytellers. Both work in the original, oral tradition. In this tradition a story is planned and told *before* being written down. The end result is not a 'reading' of a script, but a live telling drawn from memory. This gives the language you hear in *War with Troy* a unique clarity and quality, developed with children in mind. The power and excitement of the oral story remains; similes and images from Homer's original are used. Yet *War with Troy* has a narrative simplicity that makes it accessible to contemporary children.

The fourth reason is this story's cultural importance. Homer's *Iliad* was the first European epic to be written down, some 2800 years ago, though it had been told orally for centuries before that. Since then it has embedded itself in everyday language and popular culture. For instance, many children know the story of the 'Wooden Horse of Troy' or the term 'Achilles' heel'. Some will have heard of the character, Odysseus. The *Iliad*'s antiquity, length and quality means that characters and events from it appear in numerous works of European and world literature, art and music.

The fifth reason is historical. European language, laws, and civilisation rest upon the legacy of ancient Greece and Rome. Yet the current National Curriculum in England stipulates only one occasion that children have to study these societies – Key Stage 2 National Curriculum history. Even there, although many Key Stage 2 teachers use 'stories' in history teaching, appropriate spoken versions are rare. This production helps fill that gap. Teachers at Key Stages 3 and 4 also find spoken stories useful. *War with Troy* has been successfully used across the nine to sixteen age-range.

Finally, humans have always used stories to help think about experience, to entertain groups and to educate children. This story aims to achieve these things and more. As Philip Pullman told us, whilst commenting on *War with Troy*:

> The art of storytelling is something that connects us in a profound way with our earliest ancestors. It is one of the most important, most humane, most liberating and most democratic things that human beings can do, and it should have a central place in every classroom.

SOURCES FOR WAR WITH TROY

War with Troy draws on a wide range of sources from ancient Greece and also includes some material from the Roman era. The Trojan War was fought more than 3000 years ago, in the twelfth century BC, according to the findings from excavations. But we know most about it from Homer's epic poems, the *Iliad* and the *Odyssey,* and Greek vase paintings, the source of all the photocopiable illustrations in the Teacher's Guide (apart from the map and the scene on the walls of Troy). Sources for the episodes where the storytellers have kept *particularly* close to the original ancient Greek and Roman literary sources are as follows:

Episode	Source
4. First Blood	Ovid, *Metamorphoses,* Book 12 (the death of Cygnus)
5. The Duel	Homer, *Iliad*, Book 3 (the fight between Menelaus and Paris)
6. Greek on Greek: Wounded Pride	Homer, *Iliad,* Book 1 (the argument between Agamemnon and Achilles)
7. Triumph for the Trojans?	Homer, *Iliad,* Book 6 (Hector and Andromache); Books 7-14 (the battle turns the Trojans' way); Book 16 (Patroclus borrows Achilles' armour)
8. New Armour for Achilles	Homer, *Iliad*, Book 16 (the death of Patroclus); Book 19 (Hephaestus makes new armour for Achilles)
9. The Anger of Achilles	Homer, *Iliad*, Book 20 (Achilles returns to the battlefield); Book 22 (the death of Hector)
10. The Pity of Achilles	Homer, *Iliad*, Book 24 (Priam visits Achilles in the Greek camp to secure the return of Hector's body)
12. Odysseus Takes Charge	Homer, *Odyssey*, Books 4, 8 and 11 (the fall of Troy)

HOMER AND HIS POEMS

Most of the story line in *War with Troy* is based on Homer's *Iliad* (the name is derived from Ilium, the Greek name for the city of Troy), which is the earliest and greatest surviving work of ancient Greek literature. Homer composed the poem many centuries after the Trojan War: the Greek historian, Herodotus, writing in the fifth century BC, put him '400 years before my own time at the most', i.e. about 850 BC. Recent research suggests that the *Iliad* was composed a little later, about 750 BC (and the *Odyssey* about 725 BC).

The *Iliad* is a poem of more than 15,600 lines, divided into 24 chapters, normally referred to as 'books'. The central theme of the *Iliad*, as Homer says in the opening line, is the anger of Achilles. It is set in a very tight time-scale. Books 2 to 22 record merely four days of fighting from the tenth, and final, year of the war in Troy, and the central books from 11 to 18 encompass a single day of fighting. Even the beginning and end of the *Iliad* add only a few weeks to the total. Overall the *Iliad* covers only from Episode 6 in *War with Troy* (the argument between Achilles and Agamemnon) to Episode 10 (the return of the body of Hector).

The *Iliad* was intended to be heard and there are historical records of public recitations of Homer's works at civic ceremonies, religious festivals, and in markets throughout the classical world. As Greek literature and culture began to develop in Athens, competitive recitals of the Homeric poems were introduced into the Panathenaea, a religious festival to the state goddess Athene. According to tradition the first written edition of the Homeric epics was put together in the middle of the sixth century BC, and the modern text of the Homeric poems was transmitted through medieval and Renaissance manuscripts, themselves copies of now lost ancient manuscripts. The two epic poems formed the basis of Greek education and culture throughout the classical age and provided the foundation of humane education down to the time of the Roman Empire and the spread of Christianity.

The form of *War with Troy* is in keeping with Homer's original poem. The *Iliad* is an **oral** poem: it was *composed* rather than *written*, with the expectation that it would be *heard* not *read*. Daniel Morden and Hugh Lupton have composed this version of the story in the same way. At no stage was their retelling put down in writing, though a transcript of their oral performance is included in this *Teacher's Guide*. They have also employed similar techniques to Homer, such as the use of repeated descriptions (e.g. Zeus the cloud-compeller) and story patterns, and the pictorial effects of extended similes.

GREEK POTTERY AND VASE PAINTING

It is our good fortune that pottery was used so extensively by the Greeks in the manufacture of storage containers and everyday jars and vases. Large numbers of such containers and vases have survived from the Greek period, partly because they were so commonplace and widespread (Greek vases were exported throughout the Mediterranean), and partly because of the durability of the material (pottery is almost immune to decay).

Many of the pots and vases were decorated with pictures and artists would often draw their inspiration from Greek myths and legends such as the Trojan War. Stylised human figures and narrative scenes first appear on Greek vases from about 750 BC. Almost all the vases used for the photocopiable illustrations in the *Teacher's Guide* on pages 87-115 were made sometime later, in the second half of the fifth century or the first half of the fourth century BC. Detailed information on the illustrations can be found on pages 117-118.

The vase painters followed a number of conventions and used standard 'identifiers' for frequently recurring figures, such as the Olympian gods and goddesses. Hermes can be recognised by his winged sandals and Athene by her aegis (half breastplate, half cloak).

Vase paintings rarely provide the only source for an event in the epic cycle. Many of the paintings can be linked directly to specific scenes from Homer's poems: for instance, the illustration on page 101 shows Briseis being taken from Achilles, just as Homer describes in *Iliad*, Book 1; and similarly **Priam and Achilles** (p. 111), showing Priam's visit to Achilles' tent, picks up on Homer's account in *Iliad*, Book 24. But painters may add their own interpretation to a Homeric scene. The painter of Hector's meeting with Andromache at the Scaean Gate (**Hector and Andromache**, p. 103), which is clearly taken from *Iliad*, Book 6, has left out baby Astyanax, whose inclusion might have made the scene rather sentimental; and has instead added Paris and Helen, to suggest, through the juxtaposition of the two very different couples, the steadfast loyalty of Hector and Andromache.

THE CREATION OF WAR WITH TROY

Summary of the interview between Grant Bage and the storytellers

The last track on CD 3 is a recording of an interview in which Grant Bage (Joint Director, the Iliad Project) discusses *War with Troy* with its creators, Daniel Morden and Hugh Lupton. A full transcript of the interview can be downloaded from the Myths and Storytelling section of the Cambridge School Classics Project website at www.CambridgeSCP.com/myths.

One important motive for conducting the interview is reflected in the nature of many of the questions below. This was to give listeners, especially teachers, access to some of the thinking and problem solving that lay behind the development and performance of *War With Troy*. The story and its recording took three years from conception to publication. Balancing the needs for linguistic accessibility, artistic validity and historical integrity, whilst retaining some flavour of Homer's original language and narrative, was a complex task. A few of those complexities are touched on in answers to various questions.

A further motive was to offer listeners some biographical and background information about the storytellers. Storytelling is an intensely personal art and most listeners are fascinated to find that live storytelling is communicated via memory, rather than scripts written on paper. Communicating some of the personal flavour of storytelling was therefore the aim of other questions, listed below (with slightly adapted wording from the interview itself):

QUESTIONS

- How did you become interested in storytelling?

- How did you first get interested in the ancient Greeks?

- When did you first come across this story of the *War With Troy*?

- How do you remember such long epic tales?

- The twelve episodes of the story were never written down as a script to perform. So how do you remember when an episode starts and ends? Is there a particular technique or is each episode a story within a story for you?

- This story was first devised around 3000 years ago and written down about 2700 years ago … Does that mean something special to you?

- How have you worked with Homer's *Iliad* … and made it your own?

- Is there anything about the language, images or poetry in the words that you've chosen that comes from Homer's original and … bits that you've added, maybe?

- Which particular bits of the story of *War With Troy* are you own, added to the original?

- Historians believe that parts of this story are true … as storytellers, how true does this story feel to you?

WAR WITH TROY AND THE CURRICULUM

This guide has been designed particularly to support the use of *War with Troy* within the National Literacy Strategy in England. The episode-by-episode notes detail links to the Year 5 and 6 text-level objectives of the National Literacy Strategy, and offer some starting points within PSHE and citizenship. Yet, because the stories in this pack have educated and entertained people for perhaps three thousand years, they are a rich curriculum resource across different subjects and areas of interest. The broader curriculum links and main benefits of *War with Troy* in supporting children's learning of English and history are:

1.   *War with Troy* develops listening, speaking, reading and writing skills

Since its introduction in 1998 the 'literacy hour' and associated 'framework for teaching' (DFEE 1998, hereafter NLS) have become central to primary schools' curricula. Although the NLS is not statutory, children in most state schools now explore and revisit its different 'genres' and 'objectives', term-by-term, from Reception to Year 6. For instance, text level objectives for Year 5 children in Term 2 are 'to explore similarities and differences between oral and written storytelling', 'to understand the differences between literal and figurative language' or 'to make notes of story outline as preparation for oral storytelling' (NLS pp.46-7). *War with Troy* provides an excellent vehicle for addressing these objectives.

2.   *War with Troy* enriches and diversifies 'the literacy hour'

The demands of the NLS can make it difficult for teachers and children to have the curriculum time to enjoy whole books, from beginning to end. The detail and range of objectives at word, sentence and text level, and its promotion of 'shared reading' as a teaching strategy, have led teachers commonly to use text 'extracts' as a classroom resource. *War with Troy* provides much more than mere extracts. As the first, and still one of the greatest 'epics' of European literature, its oral form offers children the chance to become absorbed in the detailed plot of a rich, long, and challenging story. Yet 'listening' to the whole of *War with Troy* can be followed by 'reading' sections of its written transcript. Text 'extracts' can be 'analysed' to highlight particular 'literacy' objectives: but with the added motivation and enhanced understanding of having *previously* experienced the whole of this exciting story.

3.   *War with Troy* stimulates children's imagination and motivation

Children love 'good' stories whether watching them on television, listening to them in live or recorded form, or reading them in books matched to their reading skills. *War with Troy* is a *great* story. Its range of characters stimulates children's imaginations. This is because they are both 'different' from children's experience of everyday life (e.g. the gods and goddesses have supernatural powers), and 'similar' (e.g. the gods and goddesses argue, make decisions and make mistakes). Yet listening to *War with Troy* helps children to experience not just characters and events from a totally different culture (Bronze Age Greece). It also helps them to construct the world of an epic story in their own imaginations – and become absorbed in that world. Imaginations are extended in this process, as children learn how to carry forward an imagined character from one episode into another, connecting him or her to a whole range of vivid settings, actions and other characters. Such imaginative engagement is highly stimulating, encouraging the children not just to listen, talk, read and write but also to think about a world constructed in their own imaginations. This engagement can also provide the motivation needed to help learners meet the demands of the formal curriculum in areas like literacy and PSHE and citizenship.

4. *War with Troy* **offers classroom materials to support children's learning in other areas (e.g. history, art & design, music)**

War with Troy helps learners to explore and imagine the cultural world of ancient Greece. Because of this teachers can link its classroom use especially with a subject such as history, but also with art and music. Detailed teaching plans and suggested activities for constructing an History curriculum unit around *War with Troy* can be accessed from **www.CambridgeSCP.com/myths**. These plans focus on six enquiry questions linking history with National Curriculum English, art and music:

- How and why were 'heroes' important in ancient Greece?

- What does this story tell us about how the ancient Greeks lived? (e.g. fighting, sailing, telling stories, crafts, the roles of men and women)

- How does this story help us understand what the ancient Greeks believed, and why?

- Why was Troy worth fighting for, and how and what can we find out about Troy and other ancient cities?

- How far can we trust this story – and how much of it might be history?

- When did the story of *War with Troy* start, and how have people re-told it over time?

5. *War with Troy* **offers a classical curriculum resource**

Key Stage 2 National Curriculum history is the only place where children are guaranteed access to classical history or literature, through studies of Ancient Greece and Roman Britain. Neither the National Curriculum in English nor the National Literacy Strategy stipulates the teaching of any particular content from classical Greece or Rome; although the latter does require in Year 5 Term 2 that 'traditional stories, myths, legends and fables from a range of cultures' and 'longer classic poetry, including narrative poetry' are taught about during 'the literacy hour' (NLS pp.46-7). *War with Troy* provides a classical resource for use here and/or across Years 5 and 6 in primary or middle schools.

6. *War with Troy* **helps learners think beyond 'subjects'**

The English National Curriculum for Key Stages 1 and 2 (DFEE/QCA 1999) stipulates teaching aims above and beyond those in subjects, literacy, numeracy and PSHE and citizenship. It also aims to promote 'Learning across the National Curriculum' (p.19) by encouraging pupils':

- spiritual, moral, social and cultural development (pp.19-20);

- thinking skills i.e. information-processing, reasoning, enquiry, creative thinking and evaluation (p.22).

Classroom use of *War with Troy* can contribute to these. The story in itself represents one of the first major recorded expressions of European spiritual, moral, social and cultural development. The questions it raises about war, community, loyalty, love and relationships move beyond any single subject. Themes such as fate, violence, honour, error, heroism, family and beliefs are universally significant to humans. Absorbing and discussing such questions and concepts helps children to develop the personal capacities, emotional sensibility and thinking skills and approaches that 'Learning Across the National Curriculum' demands. Children have a right of access to such universally important materials: they also possess a natural curiosity with which to explore them.

TEACHING NOTES

Using the CDs & photocopiable illustrations

The CDs

The twelve episodes of *War with Troy*, and an interview with its two storytellers, are contained on three CDs. The total playing time of *War with Troy* is approximately three hours, with individual episodes varying in length from 9 to 17 minutes. Each episode starts with a woman's voice announcing the episode title, followed by a gong. A gong is also used to signal the end of each episode.

The episodes are themselves divided into two, three or four 'tracks'. The display panel of your CD player will show which track is playing. The episodes have been divided into tracks to offer teachers the chance to plan pauses for discussion, questions, explanation, etc.. If such a pause is not needed, the story naturally moves on to the next 'track' within a few seconds – and the listener remains unaware that a pause was even possible.

Preparing children to listen

In most classes children's experience of listening to the spoken word will vary, and some children may have had very little. It is therefore helpful if the process of listening to *War with Troy* is given status and explanation. Children may benefit from hearing an episode each, or every other day, over a concentrated period of 3-4 weeks. The listening experience can then become more vivid and stimulating, focused on understanding and identifying with the narrative rather than simply 'recalling'. Listening routines can also be established.

Learning to listen is an important element in the National Literacy Strategy and National Curriculum for English, as is an emphasis on opportunities for high quality talk and discussion. *War with Troy* offers the chance for both. It does so by building on teaching principles publicly espoused in the National Literacy Strategy. These are that 'the most successful teaching' is:

- discursive – characterised by high quality oral work
- interactive – pupils' contributions are encouraged, expected and extended
- well-paced – there is a sense of urgency, driven by the need to make progress and succeed
- confident – teachers have a clear understanding of the objectives
- ambitious – there is optimism about and high expectations of success (NLS p.8)

The twelve episodes of *War with Troy*, each broken into tracks, offer ready-made lessons based on these five principles. The following guidance also helps manage classrooms for optimum listening and high quality responses.

- Make sure children can sit comfortably at their desk, or in a carpeted area, without disturbing other children or needing to fetch things. Listening to an episode and associated learning activities will take up to sixty minutes.
- If notes are not being taken, clear desks of paper, pens, etc..
- Test your CD player to see what volume setting is needed for all children to hear clearly. Tell children in advance how long an episode will last.
- Plan to avoid interruptions, either from within the class or by outside visitors. For instance, children who may need to leave the room can sit closer to the door, so as to slip out without a fuss.

- Warn adjoining classes that you will not be able to lend scissors, glue, books, etc. for a short period of time.

- Warn other visitors by putting a polite notice on the classroom door, telling them that you are listening to a story and should be disturbed only in an emergency.

- Ask children to be responsible for the above – it is part of heightening anticipation and excitement.

Such preparations are an important part of the planning process. They signal that significant listening and learning will be happening in the classroom, and that children and teachers can expect to enjoy this experience together.

Establishing a listening routine minimises distractions, while maximising concentration upon the events and language of the story. If the classroom is well organised, children's imaginations are then freed to devise individual images and personal interpretations of what they are listening to. These 'personal' interpretations are also taking place in a group: and the *group* nature of listening provides a forum to exchange, compare and extend 'personal' responses. Talking about characters, describing scenes, comparing emotions, imagining objects or events in the story: these help children to clarify their thinking. Children identify with the story and discover that *War with Troy* can simultaneously belong to them as individuals – whilst being at the centre of a significant and exciting group experience.

THE PHOTOCOPIABLE ILLUSTRATIONS

War with Troy has been developed in the oral tradition (pp. 7-10), with the aim of increasing children's capacity to listen, speak and imagine (pp. 11-12). Its language and narrative structure enable children to construct mental images in their mind's eye, of the events and characters described. This can be enhanced by the use of authentic visual images, fifteen of which are included in the *Teacher's Guide* (pp. 87-115). All but two of these are based on decorations from ancient Greek vases (see pp. 117-118 for detailed information). The illustrations are presented as simplified line drawings for convenient photocopying, projection and comprehension.

At a general level they can be used to:

- improve children's observational skills

- develop children's ability to describe what they see

- encourage children's appreciation of the artist's style and expertise

- provide a starting point for children's own artwork

The illustrations can also be used to promote children's understanding of the main scenes and characters in *War with Troy*. For instance, when displayed on an overhead projector, they provide opportunities to:

- review what has happened in the previous episode

- predict what will happen in the next episode

- imagine what characters in key scenes might be saying or thinking

- compare and contrast the artist's and the storytellers' representation of scenes and characters

- stimulate ideas for drama activities

Finally, the illustrations provide historical evidence for the Trojan War (see p. 9), and can stimulate 'historical' questions. If so, it should be noted that almost all the illustrations are based on vases made at least 600 years after the Trojan War. They were decorated by craftsmen who lived in a very different world from that of the heroic age of the Trojan War. The vase painters re-worked Homer's story to suit the medium in which they were working and to reflect their own understanding of scenes and characters. Taking this into account, teachers can use the 'historical' origin of the illustrations as a starting point for questions such as:

- What can we learn from these illustrations about the ancient Greek gods and goddesses? Ancient Greek warfare? Ancient Greek clothing and weapons?

- Are these illustrations proof that this story 'really happened'?

- How and why did pictures from this story end up on vases made 700 years after the Trojan War?

SAMPLE ILLUSTRATION AND NOTE

Brief notes are provided for each photocopiable illustration. To help with duplication these notes have been kept separate from the illustrations and can be found on pages 117-118. The notes have information on the original source of the drawing, together with identification of characters, where possible, and key points for discussion. So, for example, **The judgement of Paris** (p. 91):

Based on a vase from Vulci, c. 520 BC. British Museum, London.

On the right we can see Paris, ready to choose the winner of the golden apple. He is holding a lyre (linking him perhaps to Apollo, god of music as well as archery, and the protector of Troy). On his left stands Hermes, the messenger of the gods, who can be recognised by his staff, traveller's hat and winged sandals. Hermes looks as though he is introducing to Paris the three goddesses on his left. Of the goddesses only Athene can be identified, by her snake-trimmed aegis (breastplate) and helmet; the other two are Hera and Athene.

LESSON PLANNING

Episode-by-episode teaching notes follow on from this section. At the top of each is an introduction that gives information about the **tracks**, possible pause points and pace for this episode, any **illustrations** (pp. 87-115) to go with it and its **total running time**. This is followed by a **summary** of what happens in the episode, divided into two, three or four tracks.

These tracks are not noticeable during the telling of the story, other than by a slightly longer than average silence. These gaps between tracks provide an opportunity to stop and ask questions, or to clarify what is happening: but an opportunity that need not be taken. In the transcript (pp. 44-85) the tracks are indicated by sub-headings.

As a general rule, it is suggested that you use the tracks to pause the action more at the beginning of *War with Troy*, when children are less familiar with the story and with listening to a disembodied voice. As their knowledge and interest grow it might be helpful to offer longer periods of listening, to develop sustained interest and concentration. But teaching and learning are complex activities and it is a matter of teachers making judgements for each class and context.

Additionally, CDs offer the chance to pause at any time, to help teachers demonstrate and discuss a particular literary technique or other learning objective, through an example from the story. It is not recommended to do this during children's first hearing of an episode, since it interrupts the narrative flow and restricts children's enjoyment and understanding. But using the transcripts (pp. 44-85) and previous listening as a guide, it is straightforward to locate and repeat a section in a particular track for subsequent discussion and analysis.

Following on from the **illustrations**, **total running time**, **summary** and **tracks** in the episode-by-episode teaching notes are a collection of **starting points** and **follow-up** for teaching. The **starting points** offer a summary of main points or questions arising from the previous episode. They also signal things for children to listen out for in the forthcoming episode. The **follow-up** offers a range of teaching points, questions and ideas or activities, often referenced to particular literacy objectives in the NLS. At the end of the notes for each episode are further, mostly discussion-led suggestions for linking to appropriate Key Stage 2 PSHE and citizenship points from the National Curriculum in England (NC Guidelines or QCA Scheme of Work).

It is important to take time over listening and discussion. This will pay dividends later on, as the story becomes more complex and your expectations grow perhaps more demanding. Accordingly the **starting points** and **follow-up** provide a variety of questions to help teachers differentiate, and to keep all children involved. Some are recall questions, usually more literal, while others are more complex and stimulate a degree of insight and understanding of literary conventions and/or relationships.

Finally, a useful way to support children's listening in the opening episodes is to develop a large family tree of gods and goddesses and/or of mortals. Illustrations can be taken from this guide (pp. 87-115), reference books, and/or children can research their own detailed drawings. Respective families and groups (e.g. Greeks, Trojans, gods and goddesses) can be extended as more characters are introduced, and as needs arise. The results can be added to and displayed each time you listen, giving children a visual focus, reminder and discussion point.

Episode 1 – An apple for a goddess

The curriculum time you allow for listening to each episode will depend on the experience of the class and your judgement as to their progress. Think seriously about pausing at the end of each track, *especially in the early episodes*. The use of these pause points will help you to manage children's listening. (See teaching notes on pages 14-16 for further guidance on listening.)

Illustrations for this episode: Peleus and Thetis (p.87)

Eris (p.89)

Total running time: 16:08

Summary

Peleus wins his bride (🕒 6:16)   CD 1 track 1

Zeus, King of the Greek gods, falls in love with an immortal sea-nymph called Thetis. But a prophecy warns that if she should have a son, that son will become greater than the father. So Zeus makes Peleus, a Greek king who loves fighting wars, fall in love with Thetis. Peleus wins Thetis' hand, but not without a struggle.

The wedding of Peleus and Thetis (🕒 6:11)   CD 1 track 2

All the gods attend the wedding of Peleus and Thetis, bringing splendid presents. Eris, goddess of arguing, is the only immortal not invited, so she drops amongst the wedding guests a golden apple with an inscription "To The Fairest". This causes a serious argument between Hera (wife of Zeus), Athene (daughter of Zeus, goddess of war and wisdom), and Aphrodite (goddess of love and beauty), and gives Zeus a headache.

The birth and childhood of Achilles (🕒 3:41)   CD 1 track 3

Peleus and Thetis have a baby boy, Achilles. Thetis is warned by an oracle that if Achilles ever goes to war he will win glory but die young. Afraid, Thetis dips baby Achilles into the River Styx in the Underworld so making him invulnerable (except on his heel). Aged 12, he is secretly stolen away by his mother who is still fearful of the prophecy that he will die young if he goes to war. She disguises him as a girl and hides him amongst women on an Aegean island, Skyros. There he becomes 'best friends' with the warrior Patroclus.

Starting points

Offer some background information about the origin of this story (see pages 7-9) and encourage children to remember questions to ask at the next pause point. Begin with something like this:

"Listen carefully to this first episode of *War with Troy*. The whole story is told in twelve episodes. Today we'll be listening to Episode 1, told by the storyteller Daniel Morden. Here are two questions to think about while you are listening:

- Daniel will tell us about two brothers, one giving advice to the other. After the episode can you say who these brothers are, and what the advice is?

- Three gods and a sea-nymph are described through the appearance of their eyes. Which immortals are also described in this way, and how are their eyes described?

"I am going to play the CD up to the end of the first track – about six minutes. Listen carefully. Don't try to answer the questions until Daniel has finished speaking and we can talk about it together."

Alternatively, you may prefer to let children listen with more open questions in mind e.g. a general question about the names of the main characters, whether they are mortal or immortal, whether this story is like any other they have heard.

FOLLOW-UP

- Discuss the relationship between Zeus and Poseidon. (*They are brothers*.)

- Did Poseidon give good advice? At this point in the story can you actually tell? (NLS 5:1:9, active attitude to reading)

- Which instruments can you hear at the beginning of the episode? (*A gong and a drum*.) How does this music make you feel? What kind of story do you expect to hear? Why? (NLS 5:2:1, features of myths)

- At the beginning Daniel, the storyteller, gives an instruction. What is it? (*He tells us to imagine*.) Why does he repeat this? What effect does it have on you? (NLS 6:2:8, success of text)

- Discuss the illustration, **Peleus and Thetis** (p. 87), which shows an ancient Greek artist's representation of Thetis' transformations. Is that how you imagined Thetis? Why do you think the setting and Thetis herself are not described in detail in the story? What reason could the storyteller have for this? (*It allows listeners to use their imagination*.) (NLS 5:2:3, storytelling)

- Some of the immortals are described with reference to their eyes only. What the eyes of each god/goddess are like? (*Owl-eyed Athene, ox-eyed Hera, red-eyed Ares, the pebble eyes of Thetis*.) What do we learn about these gods from these brief descriptions? (NLS 5:1:3, presentation of characters)

- Where else have you heard of an apple being used to trick or tempt someone? (*Adam and Eve/Snow White*.) (NLS 5:2:1, features of myths)

- Show the class the illustration, **Eris** (p. 89). What is the artist trying to suggest about her character? (*Eris is always on the move: she has both wings and winged feet, and she is shown in a running pose*.) Is it a fair portrayal of the goddess of arguing? Ask the class to draw their own picture of Eris.

- Can anybody recall the wedding gifts and who gave them? (*Athene, a spear; Ares, a golden breastplate; Aphrodite, the ring; Poseidon, four horses; Zeus, the Myrmidons; Hades, the black funeral urn*.)

- How do things change at the wedding after the gift of the apple? (*The dancing is no longer graceful, gods and mortals are no longer in harmony, the music is drowned out by the sound of argument*.)

- What prophecies are made about Achilles? (*He will be greater than his father; he will die young*.)

- Describe and/or draw the ring that Achilles gives to Patroclus. How did Thetis acquire this ring? (*It was given to her as a wedding present by Aphrodite*.)

PSHE & CITIZENSHIP

Zeus intervenes to make Thetis and Peleus marry. What do the children think about this? What sort of power do and should the gods have over the mortals in this story?

Did Thetis and Peleus have a choice? Is it always better to choose a partner? (NC Guidelines 4c, developing good relationships)

EPISODE 2 – CHOICES

Again, use your judgement as to pace. Your class may benefit from pausing at the ends of track 4 and 5 in Episode 2. Or, now that they are more familiar with the characters, perhaps they could listen straight through to the end of this episode. If you choose to listen without interruption ask some leading questions at the start to focus children's attention. If you choose to pause you can do so at the first pause point, in order to recall more easily the features and incidents which occur at the beginning. Or you may opt for the second pause and discuss the choice made by Paris.

Illustration for this episode: The judgement of Paris (p. 91)

Total running time: 13:17

SUMMARY

Priam and Hecuba's choice (⊕ 4:10)   **CD 1 track 4**

In Troy, King Priam and Queen Hecuba are expecting a baby. Hecuba dreams she gives birth to a flaming torch which burns down the city. Priests warn that if the baby grows to manhood he will cause the destruction of Troy. When the baby is born, King Priam orders the baby boy to be killed, but the baby is so beautiful that no one has the heart to kill him.

Paris' choice (⊕ 4:28)   **CD 1 track 5**

Because Paris is so beautiful, Zeus chooses him to decide which of the three goddesses – Hera, Athene or Aphrodite – should be awarded the golden apple. Each goddess tries to bribe Paris: Hera promises to make him a great king; Athene promises to make him invincible in battle and renowned for wisdom; and Aphrodite promises him Helen, the most beautiful woman in the world. Paris awards the golden apple to Aphrodite. The rejected goddesses, Hera and Athene, become the enemies of Paris and the Trojans.

Helen's choice (⊕ 4:39)   **CD 1 track 6**

Because of her outstanding beauty, when Helen seeks a husband all those wishing to marry her have been asked to swear an oath promising to help her future husband in the event of anyone stealing her. She chooses Menelaus, king of Sparta in Greece, to be her husband.

STARTING POINTS

Prepare to listen in the same way as for Episode 1. Preparation for listening is important and can become part of the 'ritual' of each session. The second storyteller (Hugh Lupton) is heard in this episode, and you may or may not choose to point this out beforehand.

Remind the children of Episode 1 by asking the following questions:

- Who are Achilles' parents? (*Peleus and Thetis.*)

- How has Achilles been protected by Thetis? (*He has been dipped in the River Styx, and later disguised and concealed as a young woman.*)

- What are the prophecies that hang over him? (*He will be greater than his father; he will die young.*)

- Who is his best friend and what has Achilles given him? (*Patroclus; the ring that was given to his parents on their wedding day.*)

- How does this episode begin? How does it differ from the beginning of Episode 1? (*Different music, a different voice.*)

- This episode is called "Choices". Can you think of a choice arising from Episode 1 that must be made soon? (*Who should be given the golden apple?*)

- What did our first storyteller ask us to do? (*Imagine.*) What does the new one ask you to do? (*Imagine.*)

FOLLOW-UP

- Go through the questions asked at the start. Discuss in detail the choices made. (*The decision to kill Paris; the decision to preserve his life; Zeus' decision to choose Paris; Paris' decision to choose a beautiful wife; his important decision to grant Aphrodite the apple; Helen's choice of Menelaus.*) (NLS 5:1:9, active attitude to reading)

- Ask children to do as Hugh suggests, and imagine the city of Troy. Spend time and try to create mental or actual pictures of the gates, palaces, carvings, paintings and building materials. What kind of work might people have done there? What about transport, clothes, trade etc? Use reference material to build a detailed picture. This assists the class to build shared historical knowledge of Troy. It also makes the end of the story even more compelling as it fosters a sense of ownership and identification. (NLS 6:2:6, interpretation as a group activity)

- Could Paris have refused to decide between the goddesses? What do children think of his decision? Can we blame Paris for his choice? Hugh asks what we would have done – discuss this. Compare boys' and girls' answers.
  (NLS 6:1:3, personal response to text)

- Can the class work out who is who in the picture, **The judgement of Paris** (p. 91)? (*From the left: Hera or Aphrodite, Athene, Hera or Aphrodite, Hermes, Paris. Of the goddesses only Athene can be recognised – by her aegis (breastplate) in particular. Hermes has a traveller's hat and staff and winged sandals, while Paris holds a lyre, linking him with Apollo, founder of Troy.*)

- Whom does Helen choose? (*Menelaus.*) Describe him. (*Red-haired, king of Sparta.*) Elicit other responses. Is he brave? Tall? A warrior? Wise? Handsome? Wealthy? Helen probably had many offers of marriage so Menelaus must have been special. If she had chosen another suitor how would that change the story? Try to get the children to say what would NOT have happened as well as what would.

- It was said that Helen's beauty was a curse and a blessing. How can it be both?

PSHE & CITIZENSHIP

Think about the choices made in this episode. How many did the gods influence and how many were made by the mortals themselves? (NC Guidelines 2e, preparing to play an active role as citizens; QCA SoW Unit 2)

Think about Helen's choice of Menelaus. Would she have had the freedom to choose her own husband? Link this with the discussion about marriage after Episode 1. (NC Guidelines 4c, developing good relationships)

EPISODE 3 – STOLEN LOVE

When you listen to this episode you may want to pause at the end of the first or second tracks, since the episode has a number of strands to it. Important questions arise from the opening few minutes and, at this stage, it may help some children to highlight points they have *just* heard in the story. By the end of Episode 3 Helen is in Troy, with Paris, and the ground is laid out for the siege of Troy – and Homer's story of the *Iliad*.

Illustrations for this episode: Map of the Aegean (p. 93)
On the Walls of Troy (p. 95)

Total running time: 16:30

SUMMARY

Paris receives his promised reward (? 4:43)   CD 1 track 7

In Troy Paris can think only of Helen, and when Priam seeks someone to take a message to King Menelaus in Sparta Paris leaps at the chance. When Paris arrives at Sparta he finally sees Helen and at once falls madly in love. But Helen is devoted to her Menelaus and ignores Paris … until Aphrodite, goddess of love, fires an arrow of desire at Helen. Immediately, Helen falls in love with Paris. When Menelaus is called away on urgent business they sail away together and slowly make for Troy.

An oath remembered (⊕ 3:07)   CD 1 track 8

When Menelaus discovers what has happened, he is furious. He goes to see his brother, Agamemnon, the high king of all Greece, and reminds Agamemnon of the oath all the kings swore – to protect Helen from anyone who might take her away. Menelaus demands action, so an army and a fleet of ships are prepared to sail to Troy to bring Helen back. Agamemnon is warned that the Greeks will only win if they have Achilles fighting with them. But Achilles has not been seen for many years, not since his mother Thetis spirited him away and hid him, dressed as a girl, among women. Agamemnon orders Odysseus, a king famed for his cunning, to search for Achilles.

Odysseus' cunning plan (? 4:39)   CD 1 track 9

Odysseus sails to the island of Skyros disguised as a merchant. He conceals a sword amongst the goods he is showing to the women in the palace, and when his men launch a pretend attack on the palace, Achilles reveals his true nature by grabbing the sword. Odysseus persuades Achilles to join the Greek army against the Trojans with the promise that Achilles will become the most glorious warrior ever. Achilles, accompanied by his best friend, Patroclus, joins the Greek army.

Troy enchanted (⊕ 4:01)   CD 1 track 10

Paris and Helen approach Troy, where the Trojans are planning a hostile welcome. But as soon as the Trojans see Helen they fall in love with her and King Priam swears to protect her from anyone who might take her away. Soon after, the Greek ships land on the Trojan shore.

STARTING POINTS

Episode 3 will be your third listening session, though you may have had more if you have broken down episodes into tracks, or if you have repeated episodes. Your children should now be in the habit of preparing the area in which you are going to listen. They should understand the conditions required to ensure a comfortable, uninterrupted length of listening time.

- Allow the class time to recall the choices made in the last episode. This helps take them back into the emotional life of the story and prepares them for the next developments.

- Is the voice the same this time? Are we listening to Daniel or Hugh? What about the music? Can you recognise the instrument?

- In the first part of this episode a phrase is repeated. What is it? ("*As chance would have it – if there is such a thing as chance when three goddesses are watching any human being*".) Why do you think it is repeated? (*Emphasis*.)

FOLLOW-UP

- Discuss the different qualities of the storytellers' voices. What does each bring to the storytelling? How is hearing a story different from reading? (NLS 5:2:3, oral and written storytelling)

- Use the phrase, "As chance would have it – if there is such a thing as chance when three goddesses are watching any human being", to begin an on-going piece of work in which children search for evidence about ancient Greek beliefs, gods and goddesses. Give children transcripts and ask them to work in pairs marking other examples of divine intervention with a highlighter pen. (NLS 5:2:1, features of myths; NLS 5:3:1, investigating texts from other cultures)

- Consider how suspense is built. We know what Paris is thinking as he approaches Helen. Detail builds the suspense; the momentum of the language is in sharp contrast to the description of the moment when they actually meet. Read that sentence, emphasising the change of pace in "and in came Helen." Discuss how this lends drama to the narrative. (NLS 6:2:8, analysis of text)

- What do we learn about the character of Odysseus? (*He is the master of cunning plans*.) This will prove significant later in the war. Can children research or tell one another other Odysseus stories (e.g. from Homer's *Odyssey*) and/or write them as a cartoon strip or storyboard? (NLS 5:2:2, different versions)

- Using a transcript, can the children find a story within a story? (*Menelaus reminds Agamemnon about the pact they made before he and Helen were married*.) Talk about how authors use this device to pass on important information.(NLS 6:2:1, narrative structure)

- Discuss the use of drumbeats at the end of the first section. (*They denote that this abduction of Helen has implications of war*.)

- Use reference books to find out what else Odysseus might have taken to tempt the palace women to buy from him. Where might these things have come from and how would they get to Skyros?

- Use the map of the Aegean (p.93) to establish the geography of the story. (Note that Athens is included on the map even though there is no reference to it in the story.)

PSHE & CITIZENSHIP

What would it be like to live in Troy? Its citizens were proud of their city and keen to protect it from attack. Think about your own locality and what it means to you. What do you like most about the place where you live? (NC Guidelines 5e, neighbourhood; QCA SoW Unit 5)

EPISODE 4 – FIRST BLOOD

This episode is short and full of action. The structure of the narrative and the manner in which it is told contribute to a sense of tension and foreboding. Because of this you might choose to play the CD through to the end without pausing.

Illustration for this episode: General battle scene (p. 97)

Total running time: 9:49

SUMMARY

The Trojans' secret weapon (🕒 4:23)   **CD 1 track 11**

The Greeks are immediately attacked by the Trojans who bear down upon them. Amidst the Trojans is one warrior who stands out, Cygnus, the son of Poseidon. He is distinguished by being white all over (white hair, white eyes, white lips) and he is invulnerable to all weapons. How can the Trojans lose? Achilles sees Cygnus from his ship, and despite being warned by his magical talking horses that he will die if he goes to fight against the Trojans, he goes into battle, putting fame before life.

Achilles makes his mark (🕒 5:26)   **CD 1 track 12**

Achilles and Cygnus reach each other and fight man-to-man. Cygnus mocks Achilles for being unable to harm him with his weapons, so Achilles attacks Cygnus with his armour instead and finally strangles Cygnus to death. But Poseidon takes pity on his son Cygnus and at the moment of his death changes him into a white swan. The Trojans having witnessed the savagery of Achilles are terrified of him. They turn around and flee back to city of Troy, seeking safety inside the city's great walls and gates.

STARTING POINTS

- Can children remember any aspects of the rich description of Troy that came at the end of the last episode?

- In the story, why did those who saw Troy feel excitement and terror?

- How does the end of Episode 3 bring us back to the beginning of the story? (*We are back at Mount Olympus.*)

- Ask the class to listen for the use of alliteration at the beginning of this episode, where there is a vivid picture of the Trojans' hasty preparation for war. They can either note examples as they listen, or find some later in a transcript. It may be best to do either of these *after* they have heard the episode through once. What effect do these phrases have? (NLS 5:3:10, commenting on structure)

- Ask the children to think about the sequence of events as if they were going to re tell the story. Again, make notes during a *second* hearing.

- Can the children work out if the teller supports the Greeks or the Trojans? Discuss third person narration and how this story would be different if it were told from another point of view. (NLS 6:1:11, reading comprehension)

FOLLOW-UP

- Go through the questions you asked at the start of this episode. Discuss the use of alliteration and ask the class to provide their own examples, from this story or elsewhere.

- Discuss the sequence of events. There are probably seven main events: the sighting of the Greek ships, preparation for war, Cygnus in battle, Achilles and Beauty, Achilles and Cygnus, Cygnus changing into a swan, the Greeks settling in for war. Prepare a simple worksheet for the class to use to help them make notes. Divide an A4 sheet into seven numbered sections so the children can write out the sequence. This will help them keep to the correct order in their own retelling of the story. (NLS 5:1:26, note-taking; NLS 5:2:3, oral storytelling)

- Ask your class to imagine being a Trojan child watching the Greek ships. Children may find the picture **On the walls of Troy** (p. 95) helpful. Alternatively imagine being a Greek warrior on board ship thinking of what to tell his family. As well as details of the actual preparations, include what their character is feeling (e.g. anger, fear, regret, pride, a mixture of all these). They might also write the battle scene from the point of view of Beauty watching her beloved master, or through Cygnus' eyes as he clashes with Achilles. (NLS 5:3:7, writing from another viewpoint)

- The conversation between Aphrodite and Zeus can be written as a play script. The gods talk about Achilles going to his death, and how they are both, in some way, responsible. Discuss this with the class before getting them to write. Do the gods ever feel responsible for their actions? (NLS 5:1:18, play scripts)

- This episode contains powerful images. Examine the language closely. Give the class transcripts of sections of the story. Ask them to look for examples of figurative language, simile, repetition, how suspense is built, and what effect sentence length has on storytelling. (NLS 5:3:6, exploring the challenge of older literature)

- Explore the idea of oral storytelling. Ask the children whether they think this particular version of the story was written first or told first. (*It was told first*.) (NLS 5:2:3, oral and written storytelling)

PSHE & CITIZENSHIP

In this episode we hear about Achilles' relationship with his horse, Beauty. The Greeks used horses in battle and a horse was killed when Helen's suitors swore an oath together. How did the ancient Greeks regard animals? Compare our modern use and care of animals with that of the ancient Greeks. (NC Guidelines 5a, taking responsibility; QCA SoW Unit 3)

EPISODE 5 – THE DUEL

This is an action-packed episode. If progress has been as expected, most children will benefit from an uninterrupted hearing; but it is important to judge the situation and to work from your own judgement of your children's responses.

In **Lesson planning** (p. 17) it is suggested that children keep a family tree of the gods and the mortals. It is very important to keep this up-to-date as it will help you track the characters on the Greek and Trojan sides. Display this while you are listening and discuss it beforehand.

Illustration for this episode: Menelaus and Paris (p. 99)

Total running time: 17:13

SUMMARY

Paris lays down a challenge (⊕ 7:43)   CD 1 track 13

On the shore the Greeks set up a camp as big as a city, as the Trojans look on. Finally the Greek army comes out of its camp, thousands of men ready for war. The Trojan army comes out of the city and the two armies face each other.

Paris, the cause of the fighting, offers to fight any Greek in hand-to-hand combat. Menelaus himself, the husband of Helen. takes up the challenge. Paris, afraid, is spurred on by his brother, Hector, the leader of the Trojan army. Paris and Menelaus face each other – whoever wins will win the war and keep Helen for himself without the need for further bloodshed. The war may be about to end.

Aphrodite to the rescue (⊕ 4:31)   CD 1 track 14

Paris and Menelaus fight. Menelaus gets the upper hand – but Paris magically disappears. He has been rescued by Aphrodite, his protector. Aphrodite spirits Paris back to his bed to recover; Helen attends to him.

Hostilities resume (⊕ 4:59)   CD 1 track 15

On the battlefield, everyone is amazed by Paris' disappearance. Hector, the leader of the Trojan army, declares that Menelaus has won: Helen will be returned to him and the Greeks will go home. The war is about to end. BUT Athene has not had her revenge on Paris for failing to choose her as the most beautiful goddess – Paris is still alive and Troy is still standing. They must both fall before the war can end. Athene restarts the war by persuading a Trojan archer to shoot an arrow at Menelaus. War breaks out again. Stalemate follows. the Greeks cannot destroy the strong walls and gates of Troy, and the Trojans cannot beat the mighty Greek army with Achilles out on the plain.

STARTING POINTS

- Why was Episode 4 called First Blood? (*This was the first battle of the war.*)

- Who is the other warrior – the Trojans' 'secret weapon' – who sheds the first blood? Give a detailed description of him. (*Cygnus: "A son of Poseidon ... white-skinned, white-tongued, white-lipped, white-haired ... as white as sea foam, as white as the seventh wave of the sea."*)

- What happens to Cygnus? (*He changes into a swan and flies away.*)

- Achilles had a horse called Beauty. Who gave him this horse? (*Poseidon.*) What does it say to him before battle? (*It reminds him that, although a mortal cannot harm him, a god could.*)

FOLLOW-UP

- Give the children a transcript of the first part of Episode 5 (pp. 58-59). Re-play the CD up to the end of track 13, where Paris challenges any Greek warrior to fight him. Ask the children to listen for ways the language helps the reader to imagine the scene. As they listen for a second time, ask them to mark where they think the writing is especially helpful and/or effective. Point out how the use of lists emphasises the work done and the scale of the operation. (NLS 6:2:8, analysis of text)

- Still looking at the first part of Episode 5, consider the skilful juxtaposition of the description of the busy preparations for war with the description of the peaceful, pastoral scene. You can also introduce the use of personification here: "the fields, the farms, the vineyards, the cattle grazing, all *unknowing*." (NLS 5:2:10, literal and figurative language)

- Discuss how a change of voice adds to the sense of urgency, how the use of the verb "watched" helps build tension and increases awareness of impending danger. Read aloud the description of the Greek army leaving camp. Why is it so effective? Ask children to close their eyes and imagine being there, watching all those warriors coming to wage war on *your* family and friends. Perhaps ask children to write a letter to a friend outside Troy, describing how they feel as they watch the Greeks prepare for war, knowing they have done nothing to deserve it. (NLS 5:3:7, writing from another viewpoint)

- In this episode there are powerful similes. Find them in the transcript and, in pairs, make up some more for the Greeks preparing for war; for the Greek kings moving amongst their men; for Paris' description of Hector's strength; for Menelaus' face; for the shattering of his sword. (NLS 6:2:8, analysis of text)

- In a large class group each child can, in turn, become Paris by standing in the centre of a circle and calling on the enemy to come and fight. Someone must be Hector or Menelaus to accept the challenge.

- Show the class the picture, **Menelaus and Paris** (p. 99). Which fighter do they think is Menelaus? (*The figure on the left with the spear in a dominant position and his helmet so tall it stands outside the 'frame' of the picture.*)

- Discuss the action of the goddesses. Mortals *think* they have power but are they right?

- What is this war about? The abduction of Helen? The anger and the jealousy of the goddesses? Is it possible to identify a single cause? Either here or at the end, hold a formal debate and argue the case for a particular point of view.

- Discuss the last line. Why is it effective and how does the music add to the atmosphere?

PSHE & CITIZENSHIP

Discuss the feelings of the ordinary warriors on both sides. The kings and the princes wanted to fight but do the warriors feel this way? (NC Guidelines 2e, moral issues; NC Guidelines 4d, consequences of aggression)

EPISODE 6 – GREEK ON GREEK: WOUNDED PRIDE

In this episode we see the tension mount in the Greek camp and learn of the animosity between Agamemnon and Achilles. You are likely to need to stop at the first pause point in order to ensure children understand why Achilles is forced to give up his slave girl to his king, Agamemnon and what he does as a result: some children may find it confusing that Achilles refuses to fight for the Greeks any more and even prays for the Greeks to start losing the war.

Illustration for this episode: Briseis taken from Achilles (p. 101)

Total running time: 16:22

SUMMARY

Achilles humiliated (🕐 9:30)   CD 2 track 1

Years pass by as the Greeks sit in their camp and wait for the Trojans to come out and fight. To pass the time Achilles goes on raiding expeditions up and down the coast. He brings back treasure and slaves, among whom are two women. Agamemnon, commander of the Greeks, falls in love with one of them and Achilles falls in love with the other. However, Agamemnon's slave-girl is the daughter of a priest of Apollo; and Apollo is not happy at her being captured and made a slave, so he sends a plague upon the Greeks.

Zeus grants a wish (🕐 6:52)   CD 2 track 2

A Greek prophet tells the Greeks that to stop the plague, they must appease Apollo and return Agamemnon's slave to her father. Agamemnon agrees but demands that he has Achilles' slave-girl, Briseis, instead. This enrages Achilles who loves Briseis. However, Achilles gives her to Agamemnon since Agamemnon is the commander. But, in anger and bitterness, Achilles vows not to fight again for the Greeks, and asks his immortal mother, Thetis, to ask Zeus to bring pain and suffering upon his fellow Greeks.

Thetis goes to Zeus and begs him to avenge her wronged son Achilles. Zeus agrees. Soon the Greeks will feel Zeus' displeasure – the Trojans will have the upper hand … for a while.

STARTING POINTS

- Ask children to describe the Greek camp in detail, perhaps reading a section of the transcript to get them started.

- Discuss the relationship between Paris and his brother Hector. Do these two seem to like each other? How are they similar or different?

- Read out the closing paragraph of Episode 5. Ask what it suggests Episode 6 may be about. (*Hector is hoping that the Greeks will grow weary waiting outside the walls of Troy with no one to fight. Episode 6 shows what happens when armies get bored – they start arguing among themselves.*)

- Tell the children that, after hearing this episode, you will ask them to give you evidence of how Achilles' behaviour is affecting the Greek camp. (*Achilles is restless; an unsettling influence.*)

- What do they think the title means? (*It refers to the growing animosity between the Greeks. The wounded pride is both Agamemnon's, for having to give up a slave girl; and Achilles', for having Briseis taken from him by Agamemnon.*)

FOLLOW-UP

- Discuss the answers to the previous two questions (see above).

- What do children think of Achilles? Do they like him? Has their opinion changed? Is this how ancient Greek heroes– or any heroes – usually behave? (NLS 5:1:3, presentation of characters)

- Which verb showed how Achilles moved through the camp? The same verb is applied to something else in the story. What? (*"Prowled", also applied to the mice.*) How does this word link these two different things? (*Both Achilles and the plague of mice are hostile to the well-being of the camp.*) (NLS 6:2:8, analysis of text)

- Agamemnon sends two servants to collect Achilles' slave girl, Briseis. They had orders from their king, so why were they afraid? (*They think Achilles may kill them in his anger.*) Ask the class to imagine the servants discussing their orders. Begin with improvisation and later ask them to write this as a play, adding details of the setting and stage directions. (NLS 5:1:18, play scripts)

- The prophet, Calchas, is worried that what he has to tell Agamemnon will anger him, so he asks Achilles for protection. Discuss Calchas' trust in Achilles. How does Agamemnon show his contempt for this news? (*"Old man, would good news burn your tongue?"*) What does this mean? (NLS 5:1:9, active attitude to reading)

- Who restrained Achilles when he was angry with his king? (*Patroclus.*) He intervened in two ways, without speaking. What did he do? (*He put a hand on Achilles' shoulder; he shook his head.*)

- Why does Achilles feel he can refuse to fight? (*He never swore an oath to protect Helen.*) Does he have a point about the way he has been treated? Is there any evidence? (*Achilles reminds Agamemnon he has had his slave girl taken away.*)

- Give the class the extract from the transcript (p. 64) that begins "That night, when the sky was bright with stars" and ends with " Down that path walked Thetis." Ask them to imagine the tranquility, the beauty of the scene. Contrast this with the anger and turmoil felt by Achilles. Why does the storyteller say the last line much more slowly? (*The pace at which Thetis walks is in contrast to the quick anger of Achilles. We have the feeling that Thetis knows her son well and has done this kind of thing before! The pace and the economy of the language show the strength of this mother-son relationship.*)

- Thetis asks Zeus to help Achilles. At the beginning of the story, Zeus was the first to see Thetis. What was she doing? (*She was riding on a dolphin's back.*) Should Thetis have asked this favour? Could she have known Zeus would make it all end in such a tragic way?

PSHE & CITIZENSHIP

Discuss the qualities one needed to be regarded as a good Greek citizen. Would Achilles qualify? (NC Guidelines 2e, playing an active role as citizens; QCA SoW Unit 5)

Was Patroclus a good friend? If so, how did he demonstrate this? (NC Guidelines 4c, developing good relationships)

EPISODE 7 – TRIUMPH FOR THE TROJANS?

There are contrasting passages in this episode. You might want to pause and comment on differences in their language and sentence structure. However, there is a sense of urgency and tension as the battles rage, and so you may also choose to run an uninterrupted session. Given that the telling is now at its half way point, you may prefer to ask the children what *they* think and be guided by their responses.

Illustration for this episode: Hector and Andromache (p. 103)

Total running time: 15:17

SUMMARY

Divided loyalties (🕐 7:32)   **CD 2 track 3**

The leader of the Trojan forces, Hector, prepares for battle. Andromache, holding their baby Astyanax, tries her hardest to stop him going out to fight, but Hector insists that he has responsibilities for the country as well as his family. Astyanax, frightened by his father's helmet, bursts into tears when Hector tries to kiss him. The Trojan army, confident in victory, pours out of Troy and across the plain to the Greek camp.

The Trojans gain the upper hand (? 4:15)   **CD 2 track 4**

The Trojans break down the defences of the Greek camp, driving the Greeks back to their ships, even managing to set fire to the Greek ships. Meanwhile Achilles refuses to help the Greeks, Instead he plays his harp, delighting in his revenge over Agamemnon.

The Queen of Heaven, Hera, is alarmed at the turn of events. How can she help the Greeks fight back against the Trojans whom she despises? She first diverts Zeus' attention away from the battle by seducing him and letting him fall asleep. Then she goes to the Greek Patroclus, Achilles' best friend, and fills him with courage.

Borrowed armour (🕐 3:30)   **CD 2 track 5**

Immediately Patroclus knows what he must do. He goes to Achilles and begs to be allowed to wear Achilles' armour. Achilles agrees. Patroclus re-enters the battle wearing the armour of Achilles, and the Trojans, believing mighty Achilles to be back fighting, flee in panic back to Troy. The Greeks are saved.

STARTING POINTS

- Ask the class to tell you about the progress of the war so far. Ask for a brief resumé of Achilles' story. Who has intervened to help? (*Thetis and Zeus who has acted on her request.*)

- Do the children feel the tension is mounting, that something awful is going to happen? If so, why?

- Ask them to think back to when Zeus got involved. Is this significant? How did Hera know Thetis had visited Zeus? (*She smelt fish.*) How do we know Hera doesn't like her? (*She referred to her impersonally as "that Thetis".*) What is her reason? (*Zeus once desired Thetis.*)

- Show the class the illustration, **Hector and Andromache** (p. 103). What does the arrangement of the figures (Helen and Paris on the left; Andromache and Hector in the middle; Hector's servant on the right) tell us about the character of Hector? (*Hector and Andromache centre stage, looking fondly into each other's eyes; Hector's fighting prowess emphasised by the massive shield.*) Who is missing from the scene as described on the CD? (*Hector and Andomache's son, Astyanax.*) Why do you think he has been left out?

- What do the children think of Hector, Prince of Troy? How is he similar or dissimilar to Achilles? To Menelaus? To Agamemnon? Try to elicit responses that refer to Hector's qualities as a son and father. Would a good husband tell his wife that he is married to the land as well as to her? What does he mean? Should Hector have stayed with his family or fought to protect his city? Hector is seen as a family man. Does that alter the way we think about him?

- Andromache is desperate to keep Hector away from Achilles. What is her reason? What does she call Achilles? (*"A wild animal"*, *because her parents and all seven brothers were killed by Achilles*.) Earlier he was referred to as a caged animal. Do the children remember when? (*At the beginning of Episode 6, when Achilles was frustrated by the Trojans' withdrawal into Troy and refusal to fight*.)

FOLLOW-UP

- The battle is vividly described and we are told that the Trojans behaved disgracefully. Give examples of Trojan behaviour the Greeks thought unacceptable. (*They kicked burial mounds; gutted the Greek wounded; threw spears at the backs of their enemies*.) (NLS 6:2:8, analysis of text)

- In this episode we see the battle between the two armies clearly from both points of view. How was the destruction of the palisade described? (*A sandcastle kicked by a child, as if a god had stomped on it*.) The victory of the Trojans is described triumphantly but the defeat of the Greeks is described as horrific. Why are they described so differently? This is an opportunity to discuss propaganda; how different viewpoints mean the same outcome can seem different; how both descriptions might contain elements of the truth. (NLS 5:3:18, personal commentary)

- Ask the class to imagine they have witnessed the battle and are writing a media report of the event. They must choose which side they are on, or 'no side': but must not disclose this to the others. Children guess the different allegiances when reports are read out. (NLS 5:2:14, notes for storytelling; NLS 6:1:16, journalistic style)

- Hera tricks Zeus into sleep and then visits Patroclus. What has made her invisible? (*Aphrodite's girdle of love and desire*.) What does she do? (*She fills Patroclus with courage so he puts on the armour of Achilles*.) Ask the children for a detailed description of this armour.

- What does Achilles keep for Patroclus until he returns? (*The ring Achilles had given him*.) Who first gave that ring to Achilles? (*It was given to him by Thetis who had been given it as a wedding present by Aphrodite*.)

PSHE & CITIZENSHIP

Is there a "proper" way to fight a war? The Greeks thought the Trojans had behaved badly. They had broken the rules of warfare. How do the children feel about this? (NC Guidelines 2e, playing an active role as a citizen)

EPISODE 8 – NEW ARMOUR FOR ACHILLES

There is only one pause point in this episode. It comes at a decisive moment when Hector rides out of the gates of Troy to meet the Greeks. You may want to pause here and discuss Apollo's interference, and his responsibility for what is about to happen.

Illustrations for this episode: Achilles' new armour (p. 105)

Total running time: 10:53

SUMMARY

Track 6: Zeus awakes (⊕ 4:38)   **CD 2 track 6**

Patroclus, wearing Achilles' armour, drives all the Trojans out of the Greek camp and right back to the city of Troy. Even Hector flees. Zeus wakes up to find his plan in disarray. He sees Hera and Athene, the two Trojan-hating goddesses, urging the Greeks onwards against the Trojans. Furious, Zeus orders them off the battlefield and commands Trojan-loving Apollo to help Hector and the Trojans. Hector, inspired by Apollo, summons the courage to go out again from the safety of Troy and face his enemy. Hector kills Patroclus.

Track 7: Hephaestus to the rescue (⊕ 6:15)   **CD 2 track 7**

Achilles is overcome with grief at the death of his close friend Patroclus. He vows to kill Hector in revenge, but first he needs armour. Achilles' mother, Thetis, visits the god of metalworking, Hephaestus, and persuades him to make a magnificent new suit of armour for Achilles.

STARTING POINTS

Remind the children of the scene with Hector and Andromache and of Andromache's reason for fearing Achilles. (*He had killed her family.*)

- What was the name of Hector's son? (*Astyanax.*) What had he been afraid of? (*Hector's feathered helmet.*) When Hector lifted Astyanax up to Zeus, what did he say? (*"May this child grow up to be greater than his father."*) How did Zeus respond? (*He did not bow his head in assent.*) What might this mean?

- Who gives Patroclus courage? (*Hera.*) What does he do? (*He puts on Achilles' armour and joins the fighting.*)

- What does Patroclus give to Achilles before he leaves? (*The ring that Achilles had been given by Thetis.*) Why does he do this?

FOLLOW-UP

- Which similes are used to describe the Myrmidons and Patroclus? (*Myrmidons like angry wasps; Patroclus like a hawk.*) Can the class find other examples of how actions and people are compared to animals? Give eight groups an episode each and ask each group to make a list of similes used. As an extension exercise the class can work in groups to make up some of their own similes and metaphors (NLS 5:1:17, writing metaphors)

- What are the two ways that Achilles hears of Patroclus' death? (*A thousand voices; the ring bleeds.*)

- When Odysseus goes to Achilles what does he see? The class can read the transcript on page 71. Why does Odysseus run away from Achilles? (*He is filled with pity for him.*) (NLS 6:1:5, shared discussion)

- Dramatise the scene where Odysseus returns to camp and tells the other warriors about Achilles, and how he has reacted to the death of his friend. (NLS 5:1:18, play scripts)

- Ask children to write a poem about Achilles' grief. (NLS 5:3:11 and NLS 6:1:10, writing poetry)

- Write a modern obituary describing the qualities and attributes of Patroclus. (NLS 6:1:14, biographical writing)

- Can children imagine how Achilles feels as he puts on this new armour? Describe these thoughts and feelings. Alternatively, write a letter or a diary entry from Achilles to Patroclus. (NLS 6:1:6, writing in the style of a text)

- Hector is described by Thetis as "man-slaying." For what reasons could Achilles, her son, be described in this way too?

- If the class has been making a cartoon strip, picture or model of the war, where would they put Patroclus and Hector now? Ask them to describe the progress of this battle. (*Three times Patroclus has climbed the walls of Troy. Three times he has been driven down with spears.*)

- Describe the shield that Hephaestus, at the request of Thetis, has made for Achilles. (See transcript p. 72.) Using this description, can children sketch, paint or make a representation of the shield? Compare it with the shield on the illustration, **Achilles' new armour** (p. 105): why is the shield in the illustration so different from that described in the story?

- Why do children think Thetis is so determined to help her son, Achilles? (*She is still desperate to thwart the prophecy that Achilles would be greater than his father, but die young.*) Ask the class if they remember what this prophecy is and what Thetis did early in the story to protect her son. (*Thetis had dipped Achilles in the river Styx to protect him and later disguised him as a young woman.*)

- What will Achilles' new armour **not** do for him? (*It will not protect him from his fate.*)

PSHE & CITIZENSHIP

How could Achilles commemorate Patroclus? What would the children do if they were him? (NC Guidelines 2e, playing an active role as a citizen) When people die now, what do we do to remember and/or celebrate their lives? (NC Guidelines 4c, developing good relationships)

EPISODE 9 – THE ANGER OF ACHILLES

This episode deals with a violent incident which marks the peak of Achilles' anger: the killing and desecration of Hector by the enraged and grieving Achilles. You might like to hear this through before you listen with the class, to anticipate some of their reactions and questions. There are two pause points, the first separating the action of the mortals from that of the gods, and the second after the death of Hector. It is important to take enough time to deal with the reactions of the children, collectively and individually. You might plan to hear this particular episode just before a break, so that individual children can talk to you later if they have any concerns.

Illustrations for this episode: Achilles and Hector (p. 107)
Hector desecrated (p. 109)

Total running time: 13:04

SUMMARY

Back to the battlefield (🕒 5:33)   **CD 2 track 8**

Achilles straps on his new armour and goes in search of Hector. All the Trojan army has retreated inside the walls of Troy – all except Hector who is deaf to the pleas of his father, mother and wife who, from the top of the walls, beg him to come inside the city. He waits to face up in battle to Achilles. But when he sees Achilles rushing towards him, panic seizes Hector and he runs around the walls of Troy, chased by Achilles.

Hector's fate in the balance (🕒 3:15)   **CD 2 track 9**

Zeus weighs the luck of Hector and the luck of Achilles, and when Hector's luck sinks down his fate is sealed. He is tricked to stand and fight by Trojan-hating Athene who has assumed the shape of Hector's brother, Deiphobus. The great duel between Hector and Achilles begins, but when Hector looks for help from Deiphobus, he – or rather Athene – has gone, and Hector is killed by Achilles.

A friend honoured (🕒 4:16)   **CD 2 track 10**

Achilles, still seething with hatred of Hector for killing Patroclus, ties Hector's dead body to his chariot and drags it three times around the city walls as a sign of disrespect. Achilles then rides back into the Greek camp, Hector's body still attached to his chariot. He cremates the body of Patroclus but leaves Hector's body unburied.

STARTING POINTS

- Discuss Achilles' reaction to the death of Patroclus, and how Odysseus had reacted to Achilles. What would or could the children have done if they had been there to help Achilles?

- Ask the children to read any obituaries or poems written after hearing the last episode. This activity would benefit from being prepared before the session, so that the readings are clear and confident.

- Remind the class that Achilles' armour will not protect him from his fate.

- Warn the class that the fight is about to happen. This part of the story is so powerful that children may hide behind their hands, as events unfold in their imaginations! If this does happen it is an interesting point to discuss.

FOLLOW-UP

If you have not used the pause points it is advisable to discuss the death of Hector straight away and then go back to talk about other aspects of this episode. The children may be shocked by the callous and brutal behaviour of Achilles. Remind them that they have heard about this before. Where? (*When he was waiting to fight and was sent away by Agamemnon. Andromache also speaks about the murder of her family by Achilles. The Trojans are terrified of him and even his own king, Agamemnon, called him a monster.*)

- Use the children's reaction to stimulate research on Ancient Greek battle tactics and weapons. (*Fighting in the Homeric era involved a series of individual duels whereas by the fifth century BC, warriors fought much more as organised armies.*) As a starting point they may wish to contrast the picture of **Achilles and Hector** (p. 107) with the illustration **General battle scene** (p. 97). Does this battle sound convincing and based on real-life events? What is their evidence for their answers? (NLS 5:2:17, locating information)

- Look again at the preparations for Patroclus' funeral. Investigate the funeral rituals of the ancient Greeks and, using the research, write an eyewitness account of it. You can display and /or read these in conjunction with the obituaries of Patroclus. (NLS 5:2:17, locating information; NLS 6:1:16, journalistic style)

- Ask the children to imagine how Achilles feels as he puts on his new armour. Describe those thoughts and feelings. Alternatively, write a letter or a diary entry from Achilles to Patroclus. (NLS 6:1:6, writing in the style of a text)

- Replay the duel between Achilles and Hector (CD 2 Track 9) and ask the class to listen carefully and/or take notes in preparation for a detailed retelling. (NLS 5:2:14, oral storytelling)

- Can children predict what will happen now that Hector is dead? (NLS 5:3:8, prediction in text)

- What are the names of the four horses of Achilles? (*Lightfoot, Dapple, Dancer, Beauty.*)

- What did Achilles say to them? Why? (*"This time bring your master home." Patroclus did not come safely back with them.*)

- Explain what Beauty's response means. (*She tells Achilles that it was the will of the gods that caused Patroclus' death, not any negligence on their part. They too are at the mercy of the gods.*)

PSHE & CITIZENSHIP

Discuss the actions of Thetis *throughout* the story. Should she have intervened? Why does she go on supporting Achilles? Should a mother support her son even when she knows that he is wrong? (NC Guidelines 4c, developing good relationships)

EPISODE 10 – THE PITY OF ACHILLES

The pace of this episode is in sharp contrast to Episode 9 and is spoken quietly and more slowly. It is as if all the anger and the energy have gone and the Greeks and the Trojans are recovering from the shock of the violence. It should be possible for you to play this through to the end without stopping.

Illustration for this episode: Priam and Achilles (p. 111)

Total running time: 13:23

SUMMARY

In the enemy camp (⊕ 6:24)   **CD 3 track 1**

Though Hecuba thinks Priam has gone mad, Priam decides to go to see Hector's killer, Achilles, and to beg for the return of Hector's body. He takes his daughter Polyxena with him and a cart loaded with gold. With a god's help they enter the Greek camp unseen and enter Achilles' tent. Priam begs Achilles to take pity on a father grieving for his dead son; and to give Hector's body to him for proper burial in return for Hector's weight in gold.

Achilles relents – at a price (⊕ 6:59)   **CD 3 track 2**

Achilles is moved to tears by the old man's pleas. Realising that both he himself and Hector share the same fate, of being cursed by the gods, Achilles agrees to let Priam take Hector's body back to Troy, for the ransom of Hector's weight in gold. Scales are brought, the gold is measured out and Priam takes possession of Hector's body. But before Priam and Polyxena leave, Achilles invites them to share a meal. Achilles falls in love with Polyxena. Achilles guarantees a break in the fighting when the Trojans celebrate funeral games and bury Hector.

STARTING POINTS

- Ask the class to retell the previous episode. Make use of any note-taking they did last time. Give the children some time to look at their notes, then ask them to retell this episode unaided. After hearing one or two versions, discuss any difficulties they had and the differences in the retellings.

- Talk about the title of this episode and ask the class who Achilles might have pity for.

- Discuss the story so far. What predictions would the children make? Ask them to discuss how they think the story could and will end.

- Tell the children to listen for a new character in this episode. Ask them to guess who it might be. If you are keeping a family tree, make sure that Polyxena is correctly placed as Priam's daughter, a princess of Troy.

FOLLOW-UP

- There is a vivid description of the terrible journey made by Priam and Polyxena. Replay this (CD 3 Track 1) or read it to the class and ask them to imagine being one of those two Trojans. What do they pass? What are they feeling? For some children a copy of the transcript (pp. 76-77) would help. (NLS 5:3:9, writing in the style of …)

- There is an opportunity here to discuss the bravery of a young woman and the role of women in the story. Girls particularly might be glad of the chance to discuss their opinions about Polyxena, and whether they identify with her. (NLS 5:1:9, developing an active attitude towards reading)

- It is possible here to introduce poetry written at the time of the First or Second World Wars. (NLS 5:1:6, reading poetry) You could also show paintings and/or photographs, particularly of the trenches in the First World War – reminiscent of the description of the plain of Troy. Use these to help the children draw or paint the scene that Priam and Polyxena pass through. You will need to handle this activity carefully. Ensure that children research thoroughly and that their rendering of the scene is accurate – not an excuse gratuitously to depict violence. This activity could be especially relevant for any class studying the English National Curriculum history unit, Britain since the 1930s.

- Why does Achilles take pity on King Priam? (*Priam reminds him of his own father and he realises that Peleus, like Priam, will soon feel the terrible loss of a son.*)

- What does Achilles mean when he refers to "the grieving smoke"? (*The smoke from Hector's funeral pyre.*)

- Who also takes pity on Priam and why should he do this? (*Apollo when he restores Hector. He has always loved Troy because Priam made many offerings to him.*)

- Show the class the illustration, **Priam and Achilles** (p. 111). Who do they think the figure on the left is? (The class will probably say Polyxena, but it is in fact Briseis, who has been restored to Achilles.) How well has the artist captured the scene? (*Achilles lies on a couch over the body of Hector, reflecting his victory; but Hector's pose is not unlike that of Achilles, hinting at the similarity of their fates.*)

- Polyxena uses her ring to pay for her brother's body. How does Achilles repay her? (*He gives her the ring that he had given Patroclus.*)

- Achilles, in a sombre mood, says to Priam that the gods "who know no care have woven sorrow into the pattern of our lives." (Transcript p. 78.) Ask the children if they know what he means. Do they think that, if Achilles were alive today, he would think the same thing?

PSHE & CITIZENSHIP

How do the children feel about Polyxena? Should she have accepted the ring? Do they think that it is possible/right to love someone who has killed your brother? (NC Guidelines 2e, playing an active role as citizens)

EPISODE 11 – LOVE AND DEATH

The story is now drawing to a close and the inevitable death of Achilles happens in this episode. There is just one pause, immediately after Paris runs through the streets announcing that Achilles is dead. You might want to stop at this point in order to discuss how joyous or how devastating this news is to those who hear it in Troy, or the Greek camp.

Illustration for this episode: The death of Achilles (p. 113)

Total running time: 12:11

SUMMARY

Secrets revealed (🕐 6:12)   **CD 3 track 3**

Fighting resumes but Achilles longs for Polyxena and writes to her. They secretly meet. But Apollo and Aphrodite, supporters of the Trojans, see the lovers and urge Paris, Polyxena's brother, to sneak up on them and catch Achilles off his guard. Paris follows his sister and spies her meeting with Achilles. He overhears Achilles tell Polyxena why he is unharmed after all the fighting – he is invulnerable except on his heel. Paris immediately fires an arrow at Achilles' heel and, with help from Apollo, fatally wounds him.

Last rites for Achilles (🕐 5:59)   **CD 3 track 4**

Odysseus retrieves Achilles' body and brings it back to the Greek camp. Achilles' mother, Thetis, comes to the camp and cremates her son. As the fire burns, Thetis remembers the gifts given to her and Peleus on their wedding day. In Achilles' tent she finds the urn given by Hades and after placing the ashes of Achilles and Patroclus in the urn, buries it on a headland overlooking the sea.

STARTING POINTS

- Achilles is now portrayed as a more complex character. Do children think that he has changed during the story? If so, how has their opinion of him altered?

- In Episode 10 there was a particular moment when Achilles fell in love with Polyxena. Can children recall that moment? (*It was when she took off her rings to make the scales balance.*) What was it that caused Achilles to feel love for her? (*Achilles saw that her love for her brother and father was worth so much more than her fine jewellery.*)

- Can the children see the difficulties that lie ahead for this couple? Discuss how other members of Hector's family would react to Achilles, such as Hecuba, Deiphobus, Paris or Andromache. (*Achilles has now killed Andromache's brothers, parents and husband.*) Use the family tree to see which people would be affected by the Achilles/Polyxena relationship.

- Ask the class to recall the wedding of Peleus and Thetis. Who gave them what presents? (*Athene, a spear; Ares, a golden breastplate; Aphrodite, the ring; Poseidon, four horses; Zeus, the Myrmidons; Hades, a black funeral urn.*)

- Just before you listen ask the children about the title. Whose love and whose death does this refer to?

FOLLOW-UP

- The death of Achilles is a pivotal event and most children will be affected by it. At the end of this episode it is best to discuss this straight away, since you can come back to other aspects of the narrative later. The class will have a spent a long time with this character and got to know him well. Children have seen Achilles at his worst and best. Give them the chance to talk about their responses as a class group and in smaller groups. Appoint a spokesperson from each to take notes and to report back. In this way you can build a composite picture of Achilles and explore facets of his character. (NLS 5:1:9, active attitude to text; NLS 6:1:5, shared discussion)

- Each group could be responsible for writing an obituary and these could be displayed around a large painting/drawing/collage of Achilles, forming the centre piece of a larger display. It is possible to do the same activity with the character of Hector. (NLS 6:1:14, biographical writing)

- In this episode the gods are busy manipulating and plotting to bring about their own desires. Discuss who these gods are, what they want and how they try to achieve their aims. If you have one, refer to the family tree of the gods. You could choose appropriate colours to show their Greek or Trojan allegiances. (NLS 5:2:1, features of myths)

- Episodes 10 and 11 end in the same way. Can the children recall how? (*Andromache is grieving over the death of her husband, Thetis is grieving over her son.*) What does each of them say?

- Ask the class to explain Aphrodite's plan. (*She makes Achilles and Polyxena fall in love so that Achilles will reveal his weakness while Paris is listening.*)

- 'Love' plays an important part in many of the characters and actions described in *War with Troy*. Discuss the different ways in which love has influenced the story, asking children to match examples to characters (*e.g. Thetis as a mother loves her son, Achilles; Achilles as a friend loves Patroclus; Hector as a prince loves his country*).

PSHE & CITIZENSHIP

What do the children think of the way Paris behaved? Who had *he* fallen in love with? Paris loved Helen, a Greek queen. His sister, Polyxena, loved Achilles, a Greek prince. Discuss the behaviour of Paris in this context. (NC Guidelines 2e, playing an active role as citizens)

EPISODE 12 – ODYSSEUS TAKES CHARGE

There are two pause points in this final episode, one just before the Greeks attack the city of Troy and the other after the brutal death of the baby Astyanax. These are significant and dramatic events. You might like to stop after each one to discuss it with your class; or you could decide to continue up to the second pause and stop there. The death of the baby is shocking. The children will be able to attend fully to the very last part of the story if they have had time to express their feelings earlier.

Illustration for this episode: The wooden horse (p. 115)

Total running time: 13:51

SUMMARY

Odysseus' big idea (🕐 4:29)   **CD 3 track 5**

With their best warrior dead, the Greeks realise they cannot take Troy by force alone. Odysseus, famed for his cunning, devises a plan to capture the city. He orders a large wooden horse to be built. This is left outside the city walls as an offering to the goddess Athene. The Greeks then sail away out of sight. The Trojans think the Greeks have sailed back to Greece and rejoice in their victory. They take the wooden horse into Troy and begin their celebrations.

A couple reunited (🕐 4:34)   **CD 3 track 6**

That night out of the wooden horse emerge Greek warriors, led by Odysseus. They open the city gates and let in the rest of the Greek army who have sailed back under the cover of darkness. The capture and destruction of Troy by the Greeks begins. Menelaus seeks out Paris and Helen. He kills Paris, but as soon as he sees his wife Helen again, he is spellbound by her beauty and she also falls back in love with him. They are reunited in love.

Agamemnon kills Priam as he sleeps and other Greeks, bent on revenge, snatch baby Astyanax from Andromache and throw him from the battlements.

A dream comes true (🕐 4:48)   **CD 3 track 7**

The gods, looking down on the destruction of Troy, are appalled. Zeus sends thunderbolts to bring towers and walls crashing down on the Greeks. As Hecuba, along with other Trojan women, is dragged away into slavery, she looks at the burning city and realises that the dream she had when she was expecting Paris has now come to pass.

The story ends with Eris, the goddess of arguing, reflecting that everything has happened 'because of one golden apple'.

STARTING POINTS

- Give the titles *only* of each episode to groups of children, to arrange in the correct order. Each group should report back to the whole class, who can discuss the ordering of the events that have lead up to this point in the story. This will help refresh the children's memories and remind them of the human cost of this war.

- Again, working in groups, give children all the episode *summaries* up to, and including Episode 11. Ask them to name individual characters who have died so far. (*Cygnus, Patroclus, Hector, Achilles.*) Make a class list and add to this at the end of the story.

FOLLOW-UP

Now that you have heard the complete story, you may prefer to discuss this last episode in relation to what has gone before, coming back to the episode-specific questions later. Some of the most important questions to ask children are directly linked to PSHE and citizenship. Because it seems more appropriate to discuss these immediately the story ends, they appear at the beginning of the suggestions below, rather than at the end (as in previous episodes).

PSHE & CITIZENSHIP

- The war lasted ten years and caused dreadful suffering and loss of life. The beautiful city of Troy was destroyed. Do children think it was worth the struggle and the pain? If they had been there, what would they have done as Greeks, or as Trojans? (NC Guidelines 2e, playing an active role as citizens)

- What does Odysseus mean by "this business will end just the way it began" (transcript p. 82). (*The war will end, as it began, with a horse. Odysseus is referring to the butchered stallion, mentioned in Episode 2, on which Helen's suitors swore their oath; and to the horse he will build to outwit the Trojans.*)

- Is it possible for someone to feel jealousy for ten years?

- Ask the class to imagine the conversation between Athene and Hera as they witness the murder of Paris. Write this as a dialogue between the two goddesses. (NLS 5:3:9, writing in the style of ...)

- Write a monologue for Aphrodite as she watches Paris die. Paris chose her over the other two Hera and Athene: so is all this suffering her fault? (NLS 5:1:3, presentation of characters)

- What does Aphrodite do to make things better? (*She pulls the arrow from Helen's heart.*) Could she have done this earlier? If so, why didn't she? What difference would it have made?

- How did the Greeks behave? How does Odysseus think the Greek have behaved? (*Odysseus is appalled and thinks that they have gone mad.*)

- Discuss Andromache's fate. (*She has lost her parents, her brothers, her husband, her baby son, her brother-in-law, her father-in-law; and now she and her mother-in-law are taken off as slaves.*)

- Show the class a copy of Picasso's painting, Guernica. Discuss their response to this and the possible reasons why Picasso painted it. (*It was his horror of events in the Spanish Civil War.*)

- Give out transcripts of two episodes of the story, to each of six groups. Ask the groups to read their episodes carefully, to find striking visual images. Use these as the stimulus for paintings/drawings of *War with Troy*, based on Picasso's painting Guernica. Ask children to think of different titles for their works.

- Display children's paintings/drawings and use them as a stimulus for retelling the story to children or adults.

TEACHING RESOURCES

Peleus wins his bride (🕐 6:16)

Imagine a mountain so tall no man or woman has ever seen its summit. Imagine the home of the mighty gods and goddesses. Imagine Mount Olympus. On top of Mount Olympus there was a throne. Upon the throne would sit father god Zeus, the cloud-compeller, whose temple is the sky. From that throne Zeus could see everything.

5   One time Zeus looked down and he saw a little island in the blue Aegean Sea. And riding a dolphin, as though it was a pony, through the shallows towards that island, he saw a nymph, a magic woman. She stepped from the back of the dolphin. She waded up the shallows, she lay on her belly in the sand and she fell asleep.

Zeus was filled with desire for her. He called his brother, the god of the sea, Poseidon. He
10   said, "Who is she?"

Poseidon laughed. "This is Thetis. Surely you know of her? Surely you know of the prophecy that hovers over her? They say one day she will have a son and the son will grow up to be greater than his father. If I were you, I wouldn't pay her one of your visits."

Zeus did not like the sound of that. He didn't want any son of his to grow up to be greater than
15   him. Zeus had an idea. He would make some mortal fall in love with this Thetis, marry this Thetis, have a son by this Thetis and then, once the son was born and safely out the way, Zeus could pay Thetis one of his visits.

And so Zeus caused a Greek king, one of the Argonauts, warlike King Peleus, was made to fall in love with this sea-nymph Thetis.

20   Peleus sailed across the sea until he came to the island. He made his way along the coastline till he found the beach. He laid out gifts in the sand and he waited until he saw, between the sea and the sky, a speck. The speck got larger, until he saw a dolphin and riding it – Thetis. Wearily she stepped from the back of her dolphin. She waded through the shallows towards this strange man.

25   She looked at the gifts he'd laid in the sand. Jewels! She was from the sea! She had pearls as big as my hand. She wasn't interested in shiny, tiny jewels. He'd laid out bowls full of honey. Honey! She was from the sea! She loved the salty, bitter taste of fish.

She said to him, "If you want me, if you want me to marry you, you must prove to me that you are worthy of me. Catch me!"

30   He laughed. He was Peleus, warlike Peleus – a great warrior! He stepped forward. He put his hands upon her waist. But suddenly, he wasn't holding a woman, a nymph. He was holding an enormous seagull. She had changed her shape. With her wings she beat at his face. With her beak she pecked at his cheek. He stepped back. He put his hand to his cheek. Blood trickled between his fingers. She darted into the sky as a tiny seabird now. He reached up and by pure
35   luck he grabbed her.

But now he held an eel, a giant eel that twisted round his arm, round his waist, between his legs. He fell into the sand. It wriggled towards the water. He put his arms around it.

Now he held a lioness that rolled onto its back, struck him with its paw, scratched him with its claw. He staggered back. She jumped into the water. She swam away as a seal.

40 He watched as she swam off. But suddenly she turned. She looked at him again with her wet pebble eyes and she said, "Try again."

Day after day she came to the beach. No sign of that strange man. One time she rode the dolphin to near the beach. She stepped from the back of the dolphin. She waded up the shallows and she lay on her belly in the white sand and she fell asleep.

45 Then, warlike King Peleus climbed out of the tree where he'd been hiding. Carefully, slowly, silently, he made his way across the beach. And then, with a piece of rope, he tied her hands and feet together behind her back. She awoke.

She knew immediately that he had outwitted her. If she tried to change her shape now, with her hands and feet tied behind her back, she would tear herself in half. She would rip herself in
50 two.

She nodded her head. She said, "You have won me."

He untied her. He rubbed her wrists and ankles where the rope had cut. And then the two of them kissed.

The wedding of Peleus and Thetis (🕐 6:11)

On the night of the next full moon there was a wedding – a wedding in a clearing on that island. At one end of the clearing two thrones – on one sat warlike Peleus, on the other the sea-nymph Thetis. All around the clearing vines, heavy with ripening grapes, gurgling streams, cattle grazing.

5 All the mighty gods and goddesses had been invited to the wedding – gods and goddesses mingling with men and women, horse-loving Greeks. Each of the mighty gods and goddesses had brought a gift.

The first to give her gift was the goddess of war and wisdom – owl-eyed Athene. She gave them a spear so sharp it could cut through the wind itself.

10 Then came the god of battle. Red-eyed Ares gave them a golden breastplate emblazoned with silver stars.

Then the goddess of love herself. Voluptuous Aphrodite took from one of her fingers a ring. She gave them one of her golden rings, a ring curved in the shape of a curling arrow, whose sharp point touched its feathered tail.

15 Then came the god of the sea, the king of the tumbling foam, the girdler of the earth. Poseidon gave them four white horses, immortal horses who once had been the crests of waves, whose father had been the west wind.

Now Zeus – father Zeus, whose temple is the sky – Zeus the cloud compeller transformed a hill of ants into warriors. Black eyed, black toothed, black tongued, black armoured, the bodies

20 of warriors but the minds still of ants. Silent, obedient, absolutely unfearing, untiring, undoubting – an army that fought with one mind. The fiercest army in the world – the Myrmidons. They were Zeus' gift.

The last god to give a gift was the last god of all, the lord of the realm of many guests, the god of the dead. Hades gave them a black urn. Inlaid in silver across its front, a picture – an image

25 of three goddesses, the three fates. The first, who spins out the thread of a life; the second, who measures out its length; and the third, who cuts it.

King Peleus and the sea-nymph Thetis gave thanks. They stepped into the centre of the clearing They held each others' hand. And the nine muses began to sing. They danced and all around them in a looping, curling spiral, mortal and immortal holding hands, dancing in

30 harmony.

I said *all* the mighty gods and goddesses were there. One had not been invited. For would you invite the goddess of strife and arguing to your wedding? From up above Eris watched. She saw this happiness. She saw the laughing, the joy. And it was disgusting to her. She felt sick. She thought to herself, "Everyone else has given a gift. Why should I not do the same?"

35 She reached into her pocket and took out something and dropped it. It fell through the sky. It fell through the clouds. It landed with a thump at the feet of the bride and groom. The music stopped. The dancing ceased. Everyone turned and watched as Peleus bent down and picked up…

"A golden apple," he said. "A golden apple has fallen from the heavens. Another gift for us!

40 There are words written upon it – 'to the fairest'. I must give this golden apple to the most beautiful of all of you!"

As soon as he'd said those words, he knew he was in terrible danger. For suddenly, standing in front of him, the three most powerful goddesses of all: here, owl-eyed Athene, the goddess of war and wisdom, her grey eyes blazing with light. She had stretched out her hand toward

45 him.

Standing beside her, Zeus' wife, the queen of heaven. She with the eyes of an ox – ox-eyed Hera – she too was showing him her empty palm.

Standing beside her, the goddess of love. Voluptuous Aphrodite had stretched out her hand. She was looking at it. She was looking at him. He knew the moment he chose one of them, the

50 two he had not chosen would turn against him and they would not rest until he was dead.

He looked from one to the other, to the next. His mouth went dry. Zeus stepped forward. He took the golden apple. He put it in his pocket and said nothing more of it. He nodded his head at the nine muses. The music resumed. The dancing continued.

But now it was not graceful, for often the dancers could not hear the music. For now there was

55 another sound, the bickering of those three goddesses as to which of them was the most beautiful. Zeus soon found himself with a headache.

The birth and childhood of Achilles (⏲ 3:41)

Nine months later the bride gave birth to a beautiful baby boy. Of course she consulted oracles to find out what would happen to her son and she learned, to her horror, if her boy grew up and went to war, though he would win great glory, he would die young. Her husband was a warlike man. He would want his son to follow in his footsteps.

5 Thetis took the baby to the end of the world. She took the baby to a dark river. She held the baby and dipped him head-first into the dark waters of the River Styx. The water flowed even over the bottom of the baby's foot.

Wherever the water touched, his skin became invulnerable. But of course there was a place the water could not touch – the place where she held him, his heel.

10 She took the child back to her husband. Warlike Peleus was furious that she had stolen the boy away. He banished her. And so the baby never again sucked on his mother's breast. And so his name means 'no lips'.

He was taken up into the mountains, where he was trained by centaurs in the arts of war. He was fed on the marrow of bears to make him strong, the guts of lions to make him fierce, the
15 milk of does to make him run swiftly. On his sixth birthday he killed his first boar and from then on he was always dragging thrashing beasts into the centaurs' cave. On his twelfth birthday, he chased a full-grown stag through the forest. He killed it with his bare hands.

When his mother heard that, she was terrified that soon her son would be taken off to some war where he would die, and so she kidnapped him. She took him far away. She thought to
20 herself, "Where can I hide my son where he won't be found? I will hide him among women."

And so she dressed her young son as a young woman. Before she left him, she slipped onto his finger that wonderful golden ring – the wedding gift of Aphrodite – the ring carved in the shape of a curling arrow whose sharp point touched its feathered tail.

For five years that young man lived the life of a young woman. During those years he became
25 best friends with a warrior, whose name was Patroclus. He liked Patroclus so much he gave Patroclus that golden ring. Patroclus wore it proudly, the ring given him by his friend Achilles.

Priam and Hecuba's choice (🕒 4:10)

Far, far away from that island, where Achilles had been dressed as a girl and hidden by his mother; far, far away across the blue Aegean sea there stood a city. Imagine the walls towering high above your head. Imagine painted palaces, carved temples, broad streets, houses of wood and stone. The great city of Ilium, the magnificent city of Troy.

5 The king of that city was called Priam – white-bearded Priam, the father of Troy, the father of the bull-herding Trojans. And the queen of the city was called Hecuba, Queen Hecuba. Now Hecuba had already had two sons – two strapping boys. One was called Hector and one was called Deiphobus. And now she was expecting another baby. She was big with the baby she was carrying.

10 And one night she was lying on her bed, fast asleep, and she had a dream. And in her dream she gave birth. But she didn't give birth to any mortal child. She gave birth to a blazing torch, with red flames and yellow flames like flickering snakes that set the whole city on fire. And when she woke up she told the dream to her husband, King Priam. And Priam said, "You must take this dream to the priests and the wise men."

15 And so Hecuba went to the priests and the wise men, and she told them her dream. And they shook their heads and they said, "This dream is a bad thing. This dream means that you will give birth to a son – a baby boy. And if that child is allowed to grow up to become a man, then he will cause the whole city to burn, like a blazing torch."

And Hecuba said, "Then what am I to do?"

20 And they said, "There's only one thing you can do. As soon as the child is born, he must be killed."

Well some days later Hecuba gave birth. And she gave birth to a baby boy, but he was the most beautiful child. His face was shining with light. His little hands were opening and closing. And, as soon as he was born, King Priam drew his sword and he raised the blade of the sword

25 above his shoulder.

But what would you have done? He looked at the child. He looked at the beautiful boy and he could not bring himself to kill him. And so he called his soldiers and, one after the other, the soldiers came into the room and they drew their swords but not one of them – even the most hardened, cut-throat in his army – not one of them could kill the beautiful child.

30 And so he grew up in the palace of Priam and Hecuba, and he was given the name Paris. And from a beautiful baby to a beautiful boy. And from a beautiful boy to a beautiful young man. And the priests and the wise men watched him growing and they shook their heads and they said, "This is a bad thing."

Paris' choice (🕓 4:28)

And seventeen years passed – seventeen long years. And one time Zeus, the cloud-compeller, the king of the gods, on the high slopes of Mount Olympus, Zeus was looking down at the world and he saw Paris. He saw this beautiful young man out hunting on the foothills of Mount Ida – the mountain that stretched up behind the city walls of Troy.

5 Now Zeus had a headache. He'd had a headache for a long time because those three goddesses had never stopped arguing and bickering and quarrelling as to who was the most beautiful. And he looked down at the beautiful young man, a king's son, and he thought to himself, "He will decide who is the most beautiful."

And he called Hermes, the messenger of the gods. And Hermes strapped on his winged
10 sandals and, swift as thought, he flew down out of the sky and he came to Paris. He said, "Paris, I've been sent by great father Zeus. And he has told me to tell you that you must decide which of these three goddesses is the most beautiful."

And he clicked his fingers. And out of the light, three goddesses appeared in front of Paris. There was Hera, the wife of Zeus, the queen of heaven – ox-eyed Hera, magnificent. There
15 was Athene, the goddess of war and wisdom, her grey eyes shining with light. And there was Aphrodite, the goddess of love – beautiful, beautiful Aphrodite.

And Hermes said, "Paris, you must decide who is the most beautiful and you must give her this golden apple." And he dropped the golden apple into Paris' hand and he was gone.

And Paris was left standing, staring, goggle-eyed, at three goddesses. But his eyes kept
20 wandering towards Aphrodite – the goddess of love. And Hera stamped her foot. She said, "It's not fair. Aphrodite is wearing her belt of love and desire. Paris must decide when he's seen us naked." And Athene agreed.

And so it was the three goddesses took off their clothes. They disrobed. They stood stark naked in front of Paris. And now Paris was looking from one to the other and he could not
25 decide who was the most beautiful.

And so Hera stepped forwards, the wife of Zeus, her ox-eyes shining and she said, "Paris, choose me and I will give you power. Choose me and I will make you a king over the whole of Europe and the whole of Asia." And she stepped back.

And then Athene came forwards, her long limbs unblemished and she said, "Paris, choose me
30 and you'll never lose a battle. Choose me and you'll be famous the length and the breadth of the world for your wisdom, your cleverness." And she stepped back.

And then Aphrodite came forwards, beautiful Aphrodite, smelling of musk and honey. And she said, "Paris, choose me and I will give you the most beautiful woman in the world."

And Paris said, "Who is she?"

35 "Her name is Helen. She's the wife of Menelaus, King of Sparta. I will blind her with love for you. She will give you everything."

And Paris said, "What does she look like?"

And Aphrodite said, "She is as beautiful as I am." And she stepped back.

And Paris lifted the golden apple above his shoulder and he looked from one goddess to the
40 other. What did he do? What would you have done? Well he looked from one to the other and then he said, "The golden apple goes to Aphrodite."

Helen's choice (🕐 4:39)

And Hera and Athene were furious. They turned on their heels. They flashed into the sky and they were gone.

And, as for Aphrodite, the goddess of love, she loosed an invisible arrow, which struck Paris in the heart. And from that moment, even though he'd never seen her, even though she was

5 nothing more than a name, an idea, he was in love with Helen, the wife of Menelaus, King of Sparta.

And Aphrodite reached down and she picked up her belt of love and desire. And she tied it round her waist, and she was gone.

And, as for Hera and Athene, from that moment they hated Paris, and they were pondering in

10 their hearts how they could bring about his death and the destruction of the whole city of Troy.

And, as for Paris, dazed, confused, he made his way back to the city of Troy.

And some little while later, his father, King Priam, called him and he said, "Paris, my son. You're young, you're handsome. The time has come for you to choose a wife. The city is full of fine women."

15 But there was only one woman in the world who Paris wanted, even though he'd never seen her, even though she was nothing more than a name, an idea. And that was Helen, the wife of Menelaus, King of Sparta.

Let me tell you the story of Helen. Zeus had many mortal sons but only once did he ever have a mortal daughter – Helen. She was the most beautiful woman in the world. Everyone who

20 saw her fell in love with her. Some said this was a blessing, others that this was a curse.

Rumours of Helen's beauty spread across Greece. Many a Greek king wanted her for his wife. They travelled to the palace of her foster father. He had an idea. He welcomed all of the Greek kings into the bronze-floored feasting hall of his palace, and then he led into that hall a stallion. He slaughtered it with his sword. He laid out the severed pieces of the stallion across the floor.

25 Here the legs, there the flanks, there the neck, there the head. And he made each of them stand upon a severed piece and swear an oath, make a promise, that when Helen chose a husband, they would accept her decision. And, if ever she was stolen, they would come to her husband's aid.

Once they had done this, the doors of the hall opened and in came Helen. All of them stared at

30 her. What was she to do? Who was she to choose?

She looked from one to the other to the next. And then she took the hands of the red-haired King of Sparta, Menelaus. Him she chose for her husband.

EPISODE 3 – Stolen Love

CD 1 tracks 7-10

total running time: 16:30

Paris goes to Sparta (🕐 4:43)

In the city of Troy, there was Paris, the youngest son of King Priam, and he was in love with Helen, the wife of Menelaus, the King of Sparta. Every day he would go to the temple of Aphrodite, the goddess of love, and he would say prayers, and he would make offerings. And Aphrodite was not deaf to his prayers.

5 And some little while later, as chance would have it – if there is such a thing as chance when three goddesses are watching any human being – there was a message that had to be taken from Troy to Sparta. And Paris went to his father, King Priam, and he begged to be allowed to take the message. And Priam nodded his head and he said, "I see no reason why not."

And a ship was prepared and the sails were lowered, the anchors were lifted. Paris stepped
10 onto the deck of the ship. The prow of the ship cut a path through the churning, blue waves of the sea from Troy to Sparta.

And Paris made his way to the palace of red-haired Menelaus and Menelaus welcomed this Trojan prince and he took the message. And he told Paris to sit down at the feasting table, and meat and bread and wine and honey cakes were served. And Paris ate and he drank. And
15 then the door of the feasting hall opened and in came Helen.

And when Paris saw her, it was as though all sensation faded. His eyes were filled with her beauty. His ears were filled with the sound of her voice. His nostrils were filled with her scent. She sat down opposite him at the table. Without knowing what he was doing, with the tip of his finger he reached across and, in the spilt wine on the tabletop, he wrote 'I love you'.

20 And she read it and she smeared it with the back of her hand. When she set down her drinking cup, Paris seized it and he kissed the place her lips had touched. And she turned and she looked at her husband, Menelaus, but Menelaus was talking to somebody else. He hadn't seen.

When the meal was over, Paris seized her hand and he pressed it to his heart. But she pulled
25 her hand away. She took her husband's arm and she walked out of the room.

But the next day, as chance would have it – if there is such a thing as chance when three goddesses are watching any human being – King Menelaus was called away urgently, on urgent business. And so he called to his wife Helen. He said, "Helen, my wife, you must entertain this Trojan prince."

30 And so it was that Paris found himself alone with Helen. And he took her hand and he pressed it to his lips. And in that moment Aphrodite loosed a second arrow, which struck Helen in the heart, and she melted into Paris' arms and they kissed.

And together they stole what treasures they could from the palace of red-haired Menelaus and they made their way, running and running, across Sparta and down to where the ship was

War with Troy: The Story of Achilles 51

35 waiting. They loaded the golden treasures onto the deck of the ship. The anchors were lifted. the sails were lowered, and they sailed away.

But they didn't go far. They went to the island of Cranae and there they lay on the soft grass, locked in one another's arms, each one lost in the other's beauty. And they kissed.

And from Cranae they made slow progress across the blue Aegean sea, stopping at every
40 single island, until there wasn't one island between Sparta and Troy on which they had not slept for a night together.

An oath remembered (🕐 3:07)

When Menelaus returned to his palace, he found his treasure rooms empty. His wife had gone! They had been stolen by that pretty Trojan prince! Menelaus travelled across Greece to the palace of his brother, the high king of all Greeks – Agamemnon. Menelaus said, "Years ago, when we Greek kings first heard of Helen's beauty, we gathered in the palace of our foster
5 father in the hope that we could win her hand. Her foster father slaughtered a stallion before us, laid out the severed pieces across the floor and each of us kings stood upon the severed limbs of that horse and swore that, when Helen chose a husband, we would accept her decision and we promised that, if ever she was stolen from her husband, we would come to his aid. Helen chose me that day. The time has come to make those other Greek kings honour the
10 oath they swore. We will gather an army, the like of which the world has never seen. We will sail across the sea and we'll fetch back my wife, even if we have to flatten Troy to do so!"

Agamemnon was less anxious to risk life and limb. He sent envoys to Troy, demanding that Helen be returned. But the envoys reached the city long before Paris and Helen, who were stopping on every little island in the blue Aegean.

15 And so the envoys came back with this message. "I, King Priam, father of Troy, have no knowledge of this Helen. But, if my son has chosen to take her from you, it must have been with good reason and I will defend his decision, no matter what the cost."

The high King Agamemnon had no choice then but to send messengers to all the other Greek kings. High, proud ships were built. Armies were mustered. Agamemnon had a prophet, a
20 seer, a wise man. Far-sighted Calchas announced that the Greeks would only be successful in this venture if they had among their number the son of Peleus and Thetis, the young man Achilles.

Achilles' father, warlike Peleus, was anxious for his son to go and fight but his mother had stolen him away. Rumour had it that he was hidden on the island of Skyros. The high king of all
25 Greece, Agamemnon, sent for one of the Greek kings, a man famous for his tricks, for his love

of deceit and intrigue, a man of nimble wits. His name was Odysseus.

Odysseus' cunning plan (🕐 4:39)

King Odysseus was sent to find this hidden Achilles. Odysseus disguised himself and his ship as though he was a merchant and then he sailed across the sea to the little island of Skyros. Odysseus, in his disguise, searched the court of the King of Skyros, with no success. Then he
5 went down to the harbour, to his crew in his ship. And he said, "My friends, I go now to the palace of the Princess of Skyros. Give me the morning and then I need you to make a great commotion. I want swords clashed against shields. I want the sound of bronze trumpets, as though you are attacking, as though you are invading."

Then Odysseus went to the palace of the Princess of Skyros. He asked for an empty room and
10 he covered the floor of that room with things a merchant might bring, things a merchant might sell – bolts of embroidered cloth, beautiful rugs, mirrors, jewels, food, wine. Under one of those rugs he slipped a battered, rusty old sword.

Then he told the servants to fetch the princess and her friends. In came the women. They fell upon the merchant's wares. They wondered at these beautiful things that had been brought
15 from so far away. They were surprised to see among them a battered old sword. They paid it no heed. They tasted the food and the wine.

Odysseus looked from one woman to the next. Surely none of these was Achilles in disguise – they were all so beautiful. Each one was beautiful in her own way.

Then there came a great commotion, the sounds of swords clashed against shields. the sound
20 of bronze trumpets. The women stood. They looked at one another in horror. Except for one. One knelt. She peeled back the corner of a rug, grabbed that battered, rusty old sword and bounded out of the palace to attack the invaders.

Odysseus rushed outside. He put his hand upon her shoulder. She turned and looked at him, her eyes blazing. Odysseus said, "You can languish here no longer. Your disguise has failed. I
25 know who you are. You're the son of warlike Peleus and the sea-nymph Thetis. You are Achilles. Listen to me! I have been sent to find you. You know who needs your help? The great king, the high king of all Greece – Agamemnon needs you to help him. There's a war coming. A great wrong has been done us Greeks and we need you to help us. We need you to fight against the Trojans. If you come with us, I promise you, you will be the greatest warrior in the
30 greatest army in the history of the world. If you come with us and fight alongside us Greeks, I promise you, your name will be synonymous with ferocity for as long as men and women speak!"

As he listened, Achilles began to grin. He took off the clothes of women, and he dressed himself instead as a warrior. He and his best friend Patroclus sailed across the sea to the
35 palace of Achilles' father. Warlike Peleus gave his son all the fateful wedding gifts – the spear that could cut through the wind, the golden breastplate covered in silver stars, the four white horses who once had been the crests of waves. The ant army, the Myrmidons, were put under Achilles' command and the last gift was given to Achilles, the gift of the god of death.

40 The black urn inlaid in silver, across its front a picture of three goddesses, the three fates: the first who spins out the thread of a life; the second who measures out its length; and the third who cuts it.

Achilles and Patroclus prepared to go to war.

Paris and Helen enter Troy (🕐 4:01)

Finally Paris and Helen reached the shores of Troy. They made their way across the plain of Troy and soon the city walls were stretching high above their heads. And, ranged along the walls, all the men and the women and the children of Troy, each person holding in his hand or
5   her hand a rock or a stone. They'd heard stories of how Paris had been tricked into falling in love with a Greek queen and, fearing that she might be the cause of a terrible war, they were going to stone her to death as soon as she entered the city.

But when Helen came through the great bronze Scaean gates, every man, as he looked at her, fell in love with her. The women were enchanted by her beauty. The children fell in love with
10 her. And, not only the people – the horses of the city fell in love with Helen. The dogs, the cats, the pigeons, perched on the gutters, fell in love with her. Even the stones of the city turned towards her in some strange crystalline way, as iron filings might turn towards a magnet.

And King Priam swore a solemn oath, by all the mighty gods and goddesses, that nobody would ever take Helen away.

15 Across the sea there came a thousand ships, each one with a bright sail, each one crammed with warriors with flashing breastplates and plumed helmets.

One morning a warrior at the front of the first ship blew a bronze trumpet. The men aboard that ship, they stood and saw what he had seen – land! A broad beach of white sand; behind it a long flat fertile plain, fields, farms, vineyards, shambling cattle. On each side of the plain, a
20 wriggling river. Behind each river, a long ridge leading to a headland overlooking the sea. At the back of this plain, a city wrapped in stone, the walls as tall and broad as any they'd ever seen. Behind the city, a mountain rose into cloud. Those who saw that sight then felt a tingling, a mingling in their guts of excitement and terror. Surely, they thought, some god or goddess must have had a hand in the building of such a place? Surely some god or goddess must
25 watch over it? Perhaps this was the dwelling place of the very gods and goddesses themselves!

The Trojans' secret weapon (🕐 4:23)

From the city walls of Troy, the people, ranged along the walls on turrets and towers, saw a darkening on the horizon. They rubbed their eyes. They looked again and now they could see a thousand flecks of mast, each one with its little coloured rag of sail. They rubbed their eyes.

5   They looked again and now they could see ships, a thousand ships slicing through the waves, each ship crammed with warriors.

And the Trojans wasted no time then. There was a harnessing of horses to chariots. There was a sharpening of swords. There was a buckling of breastplates and belts and greaves. There was a seizing of helmets and shields. The great bronze Scaean gates were thrown open

10   and, with a whirring of wheels and a creaking of chariots and a neighing of horses, a shouting of men, a thundering of hooves and feet, the Trojan army poured across the plain. And with a crash of bronze against bronze, the Trojans met the Greeks wading ashore, as two rivers in full spate, each one with a flotsam of uprooted trees, might crash into one another. So it was the Trojans met the Greeks.

15   And, if I could sing now, I would sing of the Trojans' secret weapon – a warrior, whose name was Cygnus, standing head and shoulders above all other men. Cygnus, a son of Poseidon, the god of the sea – white-skinned, white-tongued, white-lipped, white-haired Cygnus – as white as sea foam, as white as the seventh wave of the sea. I would sing of Cygnus, whose skin was charmed against the striking of sword, dagger, spear, arrow or battleaxe. Cutting

20   down Greeks with every stroke of his sword, with every thrust of his spear, while the Greek swords buckled against his skin, and the Greeks' spears glanced from him as if glancing from stone. I would sing of tremendous Cygnus, leaving a wake of dead behind himself as he fought.

One ship had yet to yield her cargo. From his ship Achilles watched, his heart in turmoil. From

25   his ship Achilles watched the savage Cygnus cutting a path through the Greek ranks, like a plough through moist earth.

Aboard his ship, tethered to the mast, the four wonderful white horses that had been the gifts of Poseidon. Now one of them, Beauty, lifted his long head and said, "Son of Peleus, you know the fate that hovers over you. You know if you set foot on these shores, yours will be a short

30   life. Not for you the stretching shadow, not for you the ripening grape, not for you the joy of children. You are matchless in the field of battle. No man could ever harm you. But a god could."

As Achilles listened, his face began to tingle, and then he said, "My dear horse, you speak so rarely and yet you waste your words. I choose death! I choose death so that my name will live

35   for ever on the tongues of men and women!" And, with a cry, he drew his sword, he stabbed

the air and he leapt from his ship.

Achilles makes his mark (🕐 5:26)

The Trojans saw him like a dancer, leaping through the air, and they saw him land, striking the sand with his foot. And, where he landed, a spring burst out of the ground. And then, as though running through long grass, he ran across the battlefield until he was standing in front

5 of Cygnus.

"Know it was Achilles who killed you!" And, with all the strength of his arm, he hurled his spear at Cygnus. But the spear struck Cygnus and it clattered down to the ground at his feet, as though it was a reed that had been thrown by a little boy. And Cygnus lifted his arms and he laughed. And he said, "Throw another one, my little friend. I know who you are. You are Thetis'

10 son. But I'm no more afraid of you than of a mosquito that I might smear across my arm. From head to foot I'm charmed against the striking of all weapons."

And Achilles drew his bronze sword then and, leaping and dancing and slashing to the left and the right, he attacked Cygnus with terrible ferocity, until Cygnus' armour was hanging from his body like a shattered eggshell. But still Cygnus was unscratched. And, laughing, he lifted his

15 own spear and he hurled it at Achilles. And he struck Achilles' shield with such force that the point of the spear penetrated the gold and nine layers of hardened ox hide. And Achilles staggered backwards with the strength of the stroke.

But then he caught his balance and, with an expression of terrible, inhuman ferocity, his lips curled back from his teeth, he leapt at Cygnus. He smashed his shield into Cygnus' face. He

20 ground the boss of the shield to the left and the right until Cygnus' nose was smeared across his cheek and his teeth were shattered.

And, as Cygnus staggered backwards, Achilles knelt on his shoulders. "If weapons won't harm you, what will armour do?" He tore the helmet from Cygnus' head. He wrapped the helmet straps around his neck, twisting and tugging and tightening the tourniquet until Cygnus' head

25 was half-torn from his body and every last shudder of life was gone from him.

And Achilles leapt to his feet, splattered with blood, shrieking with laughter. And the Trojan army stood and they stared, appalled, mesmerised.

And then a strange thing. The twisted, broken neck of Cygnus began to stretch and to curve. And his face narrowed and his lips stretched and hardened and out of his skin white feathers.

30 His father Poseidon had taken pity on him and had transformed him into a swan. And now he was lifting his feathered arms and the shattered eggshell armour was falling away from him. He was beating his wings against the air. He lifted himself high and high and high into the sky. And three times he circled round. And the only sound was the sighing and the sawing of his wings. And then he flew over the sea, over the masts of the ships and he was gone.

35 And Achilles ran towards the Trojans, with his Myrmidons behind him. Achilles ran towards the Trojans, screaming and screaming. And the Trojans' hearts turned to water and they fled. They

ran and they ran through the great bronze Scaean gates. The gates were closed behind them. And, from that day onwards, to any Trojan warrior the name Achilles was like a cold shudder from the nape of the neck to the root of the spine.

40 And, as for the Greeks, they loosed a few lazy arrows after the retreating Trojans and then they set about dragging their ships high onto the white sand.

General battle scene (p. 97)

Paris lays down a challenge (⏲ 7:43)

Up onto the white sand the Greeks dragged their high, proud ships. They arranged them in rows, one behind the other. Beside each ship they built a hut of wood and reeds and mounded earth. Around the ships they built a tall, wooden wall – a stockade, a palisade. A great pair of gates was built. A deep trench was dug, a trench that stretched from river to river.

5   This was a camp as big as a city. Each region of Greece had its own district of the camp, its own shops and stables and streets and secret alleys, exercise areas, burial places. In the centre of the camp, an empty place, a meeting place where debates were held, where altars to the mighty gods and goddesses were reared.

In front of the camp, the fields, the farms, the vineyards, the cattle grazing, all unknowing. Four
10 hours' walk it was between the Greek camp and the ramparts of Ilium.

And from those ramparts, from the high city walls, from the turrets and the towers, the people of Troy watched the Greeks. They watched the building of the camp. They watched the smoke of fires curling up into the sky. They watched the digging of the great trench from the River Scamander to the River Xanthus. They watched the lifting of the palisade. And they watched
15 the Greeks themselves, like flies around the cowsheds in the spring, when the pails are creamy-white with milk, busy about their business.

And then, one morning as the dawn took her golden throne, they saw the gates of the palisade swinging open. And, through the gates, they saw tens, hundreds, thousands, tens of thousands of warriors, rank upon rank, file upon file, foot soldiers, charioteers, pouring out of
20 the camp and taking their places across the plain, stretching from one river to the other; each man with a bronze helmet on his head, a bronze shield on his arm, a bronze breastplate glinting in the sunlight; each man staring at the city walls of Troy with hatred in his heart.

And they watched the Greek kings, moving among the ranks and the files, like stallions moving among the mares and the fouls of a great herd of horses. And the Trojans wasted no time. The
25 bronze Scaean gates of the city were thrown open. The Trojan army poured out of the city. They took their places across the plain, one army facing the other army.

And the two armies would have fallen upon one another there and then if Paris had not stepped into the space between the two armies. Godlike Paris stepped into no man's land. Over his shoulders, a leopard-skin cloak. Across his back a bow of polished wood. In each
30 hand he held a bronze-tipped spear. He threw back his head and he bellowed, "I challenge any Greek warrior to fight me now, man to man, hand to hand, down to the last drop of blood!"

And there in the Greek army was Menelaus, red-haired Menelaus, King of Sparta. And when he saw Paris, when he saw the man he hated above all others, when he heard the voice of the man who had stolen his wife, he began to tremble with fury. He leapt down from his chariot,

35 bristling with weapons. He pushed through the ranks and the files until he was standing in front of Paris.

And when Paris saw it was Menelaus who had accepted his challenge, he backed away from him, as though he had seen a venomous snake in his path and his soldiers closed around him.

And then Paris felt a weight on his shoulder and he turned and he looked. And there was his
40 older brother, Hector. And Hector said, "Paris, how the Greeks must laugh to see us fighting a war for the sake of some pretty prince! What use is a pretty face? What use are broad shoulders and shapely legs if a man has not courage?"

And Paris said, "Hector, do not mock me for my beauty. I did not choose it. It was a gift of the mighty gods. I know that you are strong and stalwart, as the brazen axe with which a
45 shipbuilder fells timber, but I will show you now that I do not lack courage. Go and tell Menelaus that I will fight him, man to man, hand to hand, down to the last drop of blood. And whoever wins the fight will take Helen and all the treasures of Sparta."

And Hector nodded. And he went forwards into the space between the two armies. He threw down his spear and his helmet and his shield, and he raised both arms and he said, "My
50 brother, Paris, will fight Menelaus, and whoever wins the fight will take Helen and all the treasures of Sparta, and you Greeks can return to your ships. You can sail home to your farms, your families, your wives, your hearths. And this ground between my feet need know nothing but the blade of the plough and the hooves of shambling cattle."

And there was a great cheer from the soldiers of both armies and a clattering as shields were
55 thrown onto the ground and men squatted on their hunkers, leaning on their spears, staring into the space between the two armies, where Menelaus and Paris had stepped forwards.

First of all they made sacrifices. Menelaus sacrificed a horse,a great stallion, to owl-eyed Athene, the goddess of war and wisdom and to Hera, the ox-eyed queen of heaven. And Paris sacrificed a bull, a huge hillocky bull, to Aphrodite, the goddess of love and to golden Apollo,
60 the founder of the city of Troy, golden Apollo who loved Troy. And then the two men turned and they faced one another.

Aphrodite to the rescue (🕒 4:31)

Those who were there wondered how Helen could have loved two such different men. On the one side, swaggering, beautiful in his prime, Paris. On the other side, Menelaus. The years of sleepless nights had not been kind to him. His face was coarse, stunted. It was as though his features were half finished. It was as though his face were the side of a mountain that had
5 been withered, weathered by the wind and the rain. It was as though the gaze of Helen gave a kind of beauty to the one she loved and, when she chose to look away, age ravaged the one she'd left behind.

But bitter hurt brings strength. Menelaus had waited for this moment. He had played it out in his mind time and again, and he was not about to waste it. Paris threw his spear first.

10   Menelaus dodged it easily and, with a whispered prayer, he threw his own. And his aim was true. Paris was lifted off his feet. He flew backwards. He fell with a crash and a cloud of dust. The spear had broken through his shield, through his breastplate and grazed the skin of his chest.

Before Paris could stand, Menelaus was over him, lunging at him with his sword. Paris had to
15   wriggle in the dust to dodge every thrust. Then Menelaus stopped. He lifted the sword above his head. He brought it down for the deathblow, but a strange thing happened. The blade shattered like a brittle icicle against Paris' armour. Menelaus gasped. He threw down the handle of the sword. He pushed his fingers under the chinstrap of Paris' helmet, and he turned and ran, dragging the flailing Paris towards the Greek army.

20   A thousand arms stretched out towards their king. Joyfully, he reached out towards them but then he fell. He tripped over nothing. A fog fell over the field of battle. He could see nothing, no one. He lifted up the helmet. The chinstrap had snapped! The helmet was empty. Paris had vanished! Aphrodite, seeing her precious Paris in mortal danger had shattered the sword, snapped the chinstrap, brought down the fog. And now she was lifting Paris tenderly in her
25   arms. She lifted him high and high above the Trojan plain. She carried him over the city walls. She carried him into his palace. She laid him down tenderly on his bed.

And then the goddess of love changed her shape so that to all the world she looked like an old woman. And she went scuttling through the streets of Troy, until she found Helen. And Helen was leaning over the walls. She was looking into the fog. She was rubbing her eyes, she was
30   looking again. She was trying to work out what had happened to Paris. And suddenly she felt a tugging at her skirt, and she turned and she looked and there was an old woman she'd never seen before. And the old woman said, "Helen, your lover is in his bedchamber. He's lying on his bed. He's waiting for you. He calls your name over and over. Go to him, now!"

And the old woman had vanished and there was a smell left hanging on the air. And Helen,
35   she breathed it in, a smell of musk and honey. And she was filled with spirit and awe, in the knowledge that she'd been in the presence of one of the mighty goddesses. And she hurried through the streets to Paris' palace. She ran up the stairs. She pushed open the door of his bedchamber. And there he was, lying on his bed, still dressed in his armour, still smeared with the dust of the battlefield.

40   And Helen ran across and she said, "Paris, Paris, never have I been filled with such longing for you, not since we first lay down together on the soft grass on the island of Cranae." And she kissed his eyes and she kissed his cheek and she kissed his mouth. And they lay down together, locked in one another's arms.

Hostilities resume (🕐 4:59)

Out on the battlefield the fog had lifted. The Trojan prince, Hector, stepped forward. He showed the Greeks his open hands. He said, "I swear to you, I swear to you Greeks by the

broad skies, I swear to you Greeks by the dark waters of the river Styx, I have searched my armies and my brother has vanished! Surely some god or goddess intervened, brought down
5　that fog, plucked my brother from the field of battle? Before the duel it was agreed that the victor would take Helen and all the treasures of Sparta. Every one of us here knows you, Menelaus, defeated my brother. Therefore you Greeks are the victors. Therefore all the treasures that were taken from you will be returned to you. Helen will be restored to you and you will soon sail home to see your hearths, your fields, your farms, your families again."

10　And there was a great cheer from the Greek ranks. But up above, owl-eyed Athene, the goddess of war and wisdom, was watching and listening. The war was about to end. Troy was still standing and Paris was still alive. This was very disappointing! She's never at a loss for a plan. In the time it would take you or me to blink, she flashed down from the sky. Soundless, invisible, she moved among the Trojan armies until she found a stupid, shallow man, whose
15　mind she could bend to her will.

She whispered in his ear, "Pandarus, look. Menelaus has dropped his shield. He has no weapons now. With a single arrow you could win this war for Troy. You'd be the hero of the city. Look at that neck, the baggy folds of flesh. Kill Menelaus!"

Without a second thought, without a second breath, Pandarus put an arrow to his bow. He
20　loosed the arrow. If we could see the way the gods and goddesses can see, we would have seen Athene reach down and touch the tail of the arrow as it flew through the air so that it struck not Menelaus' neck – it struck his breastplate. It struck and stuck and knocked him to the ground. He was winded but he was unharmed.

His men looked. They saw the arrow protruding out of his breastplate and they were sure that
25　he was dead. These treacherous Trojans had broken the truce. They surged forwards into the Trojan ranks and, at their forefront, severing heads with every stroke of his sword, the swift-runner Achilles. The Trojans, stunned by the suddenness of the attack, they turned and they fled. They dropped their weapons; they ran through the bronze Scaean gates. The Greeks tried to follow but the Trojan bowmen, on top of the walls, they loosed their arrows and drove
30　the Greeks back.

The Greeks were jubilant. They drank around fires until late into the night. Next morning they set off to sack this city. But, as soon as they came within bowshot of the walls, the Trojan archers loosed their arrows. A black rain came.

It was that way from then on. If the Greek and Trojan armies met in open battle, thanks to
35　Achilles and his black-armoured Myrmidons, the Greeks were unstoppable. But, as soon as the Trojans retreated close to the walls of their city, the Greeks could do no more. Those walls were impregnable.

Hector, Prince of Troy, decreed the Trojans would not set forth from their city. Instead they would wait, within the walls, as long as it took until the Greeks gave up and went home. There
40　were plenty of secret ways off Mount Ida through which their allies could bring food. And so the siege of Troy began.

EPISODE 6 – Greek on Greek: wounded pride

CD 2 tracks 1-2

total running time: 16:22

Agamemnon humiliates Achilles (⏰ 9:30)

Inside their city, the Trojans waited for the Greeks to give up and sail home. In their camp, the Greeks waited for the Trojans to emerge so that they could sack the city. Whole years went by without a single battle. The Greeks in their camp became restless, impatient. Old, stupid rivalries began to rear their heads among the many Greek kings. The high king of the whole

5   camp, the high king of all of Greece, Agamemnon, became worried. He could see that soon this camp would become a kind of war.

The biggest threat of all, of course, came from the swift-runner, the son of Peleus and Thetis, Achilles. This was not a man who enjoyed waiting. This was a man who loved to hunt, to fight, to kill. He prowled around the camp like a caged beast, staring, glaring at anyone who dared

10 even to look at him.

Agamemnon had an idea. He ordered the swift-runner Achilles to set off in a ship and sail up and down the coast, attacking anywhere known to be sympathetic to the Trojans. In this way, Achilles was away for years, attacking, sacking, looting, burning anywhere that nurtured men and women.

15 When finally he returned to the Greek camp, what a hoard he brought with him! Gold, jewels, weapons, tools, food, wine and slaves. Among the slaves, the high King Agamemnon saw a woman – a daughter of a priest of Apollo. As soon as Agamemnon saw her, he wanted her for himself. He wanted her for his bed. And so he took her.

Among the slaves, the only one who was a match for this daughter of a priest of Apollo, was a

20 woman named Briseis. Agamemnon, with great ceremony, gave this Briseis to Achilles to thank him for all the things that he had done during his voyage, as though that voyage had brought glory onto the Greeks instead of shame.

But, up above, Trojan-loving Apollo was watching and listening. These Greeks, first they attack and besiege his favourite city, then they slaughter its children, and now they enslave the

25 daughter of his loyal priest! The lord of light, the mighty archer, has many awful ways to punish men and women.

By night, under cover of darkness, he sent into the Greek camp tens, hundreds, thousands, tens of thousands of silky, grey backs – field mice – that brought with them a sickness that thrived on the pools of filthy water, the heaps of stinking rubbish that had gathered in the

30 Greek camp over the years.

The first the Greeks knew of it was when the stray dogs of the camp died one by one. Then goats, mules, horses began to die. And then men. It was an awful sight to see a man with whom you'd risked your life wither away, age whole years across a single day, and die. The plague prowled through the camp for months.

35   Eventually Achilles called a meeting in the gathering place. He said, "Look, wherever I turn I can see rising into the sky the smoke of funeral pyres. There is, among our number, one who can understand the moods of the gods and goddesses by the patterns the birds make as they fly through the sky. We have a prophet, a seer, a wise man: far-sighted Calchas should speak."

Old Calchas winced. He said, "Swift-runner Achilles, please, promise me your protection
40   before I explain the source of this plague because the bearer of bad news is never welcome and my words will bring upon me the anger of the powerful."

Achilles nodded. Old Calchas said, "This plague has been sent by the lord of light. Apollo is furious with us because our high king, Agamemnon, has taken to his bed a daughter of Apollo's loyal priest. Until that woman is set free, every day will see more dead."

45   "Old man," said Agamemnon, "would good news burn your tongue? Never a prophecy of victory for me – only more bad news, heaped upon the one who pays for your food! I love this woman, this daughter of a priest of Apollo. I love her as dearly as I love my own wife, Clytemnestra, so far away. But, since I value the well-being of my subjects – you, my armies – more than I do my own peace of mind, I will let this woman go. I'll let her go tomorrow, with
50   gold, in one of my ships. However, this means that I, your high king, am to go without the treasures of Achilles' voyage. That is unthinkable! If I'm to let this woman go, I want one in return!"

"From where?" said Achilles. "There are no slaves left to be shared out. You, of all of us, know that. When Troy falls you'll be given three or four slaves to make up for the one you let go
55   today."

"Why, thank you," said Agamemnon. "But I seem to remember that I am the high king of this army and not you. You are just another prince under my command. Your good opinion of me means nothing to me! But since you're so keen to make up for my loss, I will take a slave from you. Yes! Yes, that Briseis. I gave her to you when you returned to this camp. I take her now.
60   She is mine now!"

Achilles took a little step forward then. He felt a hand on his shoulder. He looked behind him. There was his best friend Patroclus, shaking his head. Achilles stepped back. Were it not for the hand of his friend, Achilles would have jumped, beaten the high King Agamemnon to the ground, torn off his shiny breastplate and scooped his beating heart out of his chest.

65   "Take her!" said Achilles, "But this means the son of Peleus and Thetis will not fight for you again. No oath binds me to the protection of Helen. I was not one of those kings who stood on the severed limbs of a stallion and swore to protect her years ago. And yet I have fought for you for years. I've waded through fields of blood. And for what? So that when finally I find a woman, you can take her from me? Well, I will not fight for you again, not if you beg me!"

70   "Good!" said Agamemnon. "Go, leave this place. By tomorrow you'd be forgotten. Just some stupid boy who's not man enough to take a command. You are not a warrior. Why the lowliest

soldier in the shabbiest squad in this army knows, to win this war, he must obey me. He must obey his king. You are a monster. I have never seen such delight in the eyes of one when he
75   took the life of another. This army, my camp is better off without you!"   And he turned and he was gone. The crowd was gone in moments, leaving only Achilles and Patroclus in their place, Achilles shaking with fury.

Zeus grants a wish (🕐 6:52)

And so it was, the next day the daughter of the priest of Apollo was set free. She sailed home in one of Agamemnon's ships with gold. As soon as she reached her homeland, the plague in the Greek camp ended. Apollo turned his glare elsewhere.

And so it was, two servants were sent across the camp, down to where the breakers crash and
5   drag, down to Achilles' hut, to demand he give up his slave Briseis. They were terrified as they approached his hut but he welcomed them politely. He let the woman go readily. He embraced her one last time. There were tears in their eyes when they parted and then Briseis walked across the camp to Agamemnon's hut, to Agamemnon's bed.

That night, when the sky was bright with stars, the swift-runner Achilles walked to the edge of
10   the ocean, waded into the shallows, sank to his knees, and his face creased into a childish sob. Through his tears he saw the shining path made by the moon. Down that path walked Thetis.

"Mother, many's the time in father's hall I heard you say that Zeus desired you. Go to him now. He could make these Greeks taste pain. I want blood in the sand! I want the ships of this camp
15   burning! And then these Greeks will remember that I was out on the battlefield every day, cutting off heads with every stroke of my sword, while their torn-hearted, dog-faced king cowered behind the palisade."

"My dear son," she said, "I can refuse you nothing. I will go to Zeus, whose temple is the sky, and he will grant your wish. Until then, stay by your ships." And she rose up into the heavens.

20   She made her way through the clouds, high and high and high, until she came to the slopes of Mount Olympus, and there was Zeus' palace. She ran in through the doors. There was Zeus himself, the cloud-compeller, sitting on his golden throne. Thetis threw herself onto the floor at his feet.

She curled her left arm over his knees and she said, "Great Zeus, if ever I have pleased you in
25   word or in deed, listen to me now! My son, Achilles, has been bitterly insulted by swaggering Agamemnon. Agamemnon has taken his woman, who he won in warfare. He has taken her to his own bed. And now my son refuses to fight. He will not lift a sword for the Greeks. He has retired from the fray. Oh great Zeus, I beg you, teach that swaggering, dog-faced Agamemnon how much he needs my son. Give the Trojans a tremendous victory. May the Greeks wallow in
30   their own gore! May they be steeped in their own blood! If you grant my wish then bow your head in agreement. If you do not bow your head, I know that I, of all immortals, count the least."

And great Zeus listened. And he pondered in his heart. And then he bowed his head and he said, "I grant your wish." And he said, "These things I will bring to pass." And he thought "In my

35 own way."

And Thetis thanked him with all of her heart and then she descended from the heavens. And no sooner was she gone than Hera, ox-eyed Hera, the queen of heaven, Zeus' wife, and Athene, goddess of war and wisdom, came striding into Zeus' palace. And Hera sniffed at the air.

40 "I smell fish! That sea-nymph Thetis must have been here. What did she want?" And Zeus said, "She asked a favour and I have granted it."

And he smiled, and he got up to his feet, and he made his way out of his palace and he descended from the heavens down and down and down and down to a rocky crag on Mount Ida, the great mountain that stretched up behind the city walls of Troy. And he sat and he

45 waited until the dawn took her golden throne. And he looked down at the city of Troy, ringed in stone with its shining diadem of towers. And he looked across the plain and the Greek camp and the blue waves of the sea, and he lifted his right hand and, in it, he was holding a set of golden scales.

And into one pan of the scales, he put the luck of the Greek army; and into the other pan of the

50 scales, he put the luck of the Trojan army. And he held the scales by the centre of the beam and he watched as the Greek luck sank down and down and down, towards Hades' halls. And the Trojan luck soared up into the skies.

Briseis taken from Achilles (p. 101)

Hector's wife begs him not to fight (⏰ 7:32)

On the rocky crag on Mount Ida, Zeus looked at his golden scales and he saw the Greek luck sinking down towards Hades' halls, and he saw the Trojan luck soaring up into the skies. And, in that moment, in the city of Troy, Hector, the eldest son of King Priam, woke up with his heart soaring in his breast. He leapt out of bed. He kissed his wife Andromache, still asleep on the

5   bed. He pulled on his clothes and his armour. He ran out of his palace. He sent lieutenants to all corners of the city, waking warriors, and soon the air was thick with the sound of the sharpening of swords, the greasing of axles, the harnessing of horses to chariots, the seizing of helmets and shields, the buckling of breastplates and belts and greaves.

And, if I could sing, I would sing of Hector himself, striding this way and that way. The leather

10   rim of his bossed shield slung onto his back, tapping the nape of his neck and the backs of his ankles, as he exalts and encourages his men. And soon the whole city was humming.

And Hector made his way down towards the city gates and, as he was walking, he saw coming towards him his wife, Andromache, and, walking behind her, a nursemaid with their little son, Astyanax, in her arms. And, when Andromache saw Hector, she ran forwards and she threw

15   her hands around his neck, and she said, "Sweet Hector, this courage will be the death of you. Achilles is a wild animal. He is a savage beast. In his ravaging the coast from the Black Sea to the Nile, he has killed all seven of my brothers. He has killed my father. He has killed my mother. The city that gave me birth is nothing more than a pile of crumbling, blood-soaked rubble. Hector, do not make me a widow as well as an orphan."

20   And Hector said, "Andromache, what can I do? If a man is guarding his sheep on the slopes of Mount Ida and he finds himself surrounded by wolves or by thieves, does he turn tail and run? Or does he stand firm and fight? I am my father's son. I am our son's father. This land from Mount Ida to the sea, from the river Scamander to the river Xanthus, is my inheritance. As I am father of this family, one day I will also be father of this land."

25   And Andromache looked at him and she said, "Then who are you married to? Me or the land?"

And Hector said, "Both, my love."

And he reached and he took the baby from the nursemaid's hand, his little son, Astyanax. But, as he lifted him, the baby wrinkled up his face, and he opened his mouth and he screamed, and tears were spurting out of his eyes. And Andromache smiled through her tears and she

30   said, "Sweet Hector, it is your helmet that frightens him."

And she reached and she lifted the great bronze helmet, with its nodding plume of horsehair, from Hector's head, and she set it onto the ground at his feet. And Hector lifted his little baby son and he pressed his nose against the baby's nose, and the tears turned to bubbling laughter. And Hector lifted his son high above his head and he said, "Great father Zeus, may

35   this child grow up to be greater than his father!"

And Zeus, on the rocky crag on Mount Ida, was watching and smiling fondly. But he did not bow his head in assent.

And Hector gave the baby to Andromache and he reached down, and he picked up his helmet and he put it onto his head. And he said, "Andromache, nobody, whether hero or coward, can
40 avoid his fate. Even Zeus can only watch as the scales of luck either rise or fall."

And he made his way down towards the gate. And he hadn't gone far when his brother, Paris, caught up with him, like some great bull that's been locked in the barn all winter and with the first strength of spring, when the barn doors are thrown open, the bull goes dancing and skipping across the flowery fields. So it was that Paris caught up with Hector, and Hector put
45 his arm around his brother's neck and kissed him.

And then he went down to his golden chariot and there were his horses, stamping and steaming and champing at the bit. And he stroked the horses' faces with the back of his hand and he said, "My beauties, today is your chance to repay me for all those mornings when my wife, Andromache, has given you honeyed wheats before she brought me my own breakfast."

50 And he climbed up into the car of his chariot, and he turned and he faced the great Trojan army, massed inside the city walls. He said, "Today we ride against the Greeks. Great father Zeus is on our side. I feel it in my bones. We will drive them before us and, when we reach their flimsy, futile palisade, our horses' hooves will kick it down and, when we reach their hollow ships, the watchword will be fire!"

55 And there was a tremendous cheer from the Trojan army. The great bronze Scaean gates were thrown open and, with a whirring of wheels and a creaking of chariots, a neighing of horses, a shouting of men, a thundering of hooves and feet, the Trojan army poured across the plain and, with a crash of bronze against bronze, the Trojans met the Greeks.

And, if I could sing now, I would sing of Hector, as his charioteer whipped the horses to a
60 gallop, every cell of his body poised, immaculate. I would sing of Hector, cutting down Greeks like ripe corn, leaving them in swathes six deep, twelve deep, behind him. And behind Hector, the Trojan army driving the Greeks before them. And, when they reached the palisade, the Trojan horses kicked it down, as a little boy on the seashore might kick down a sandcastle. And the Greek hearts turned to water and they fled.

65 And, if I could sing now, I would sing of the menace in Hector's eyes, flickering beneath the bronze rim of his helmet. I would sing of the menace in the tilt of his helmet on his temples, as he fought.

Trojan successes upset Hera (⏱ 4:15)

The Greeks, to their horror, saw their palisade, their wooden fence, come toppling down, as though some god had stomped on it. And, through the breach, there came a chariot. Behind the chariot, a surge of brazen Trojans, each one brandishing a flaming torch. Those Trojans, they kicked over the burial mounds they found. They gutted the Greeks who could not run

5   away, the Greek wounded. They threw spears at fleeing Greek backs.

The Greeks, they formed a line in front of their ships. They fought with whatever they could find, with sticks, with staves, with stones, with rocks. Menelaus was aboard one of the ships, cracking Trojan heads with a great oar. But soon there arose from one of those ships black smoke.

10 Not far away, in his hut, Achilles listened to the crackling flames. He listened to the screams of the dying Greeks. He smiled to himself. He picked up a silver harp and he began to play.

On the high slopes of Mount Olympus, Hera and Athene watched the smoke rising from the Greek ships, and the blood drained from their faces. Something had to be done. The ox-eyed queen of heaven made her way into her palace. She closed the door behind herself. She took

15 off her clothes. She washed herself from head to foot, and then she rubbed scented oils into her skin, and she found a shimmering robe. She threw it over her shoulders; she clasped it at the throat with a golden clasp. And then she set off in search of Aphrodite, the goddess of love.

And when she found her, she said, "Aphrodite, dear child, I wonder if you would do me a

20 favour, if you're not too angry with me for siding with the Greeks."

And Aphrodite said, "What favour?"

And Hera said, "I wonder if you would be kind enough to lend me your belt of love and desire because, you see, the sky and the earth have fallen out with one another. They do nothing but argue and bicker and quarrel and fight. Maybe, if I could lend them your belt, I could make

25 peace between them."

And Aphrodite said, "Well, it would be unkind of me not to lend you my belt for such an important task." And she unclasped it and she gave it to Hera. And Hera took it from her. And, as soon as Hera was out of sight, she tied it around her own waist and she descended from the heavens, down and down and down to the rocky crag where Zeus was sitting, watching the

30 smoke rising from the Greek ships.

And suddenly, out of the corner of his eye, he saw his wife and he said, "Hera, never have I been filled with such desire, such longing for a mortal or an immortal." And he drew her towards him and he unclasped the golden clasp. And Hera said, "Zeus! What? Here? Now? But we might be seen! Think how gossiping tongues would wag!"

35 And Zeus said, "Hera, I will cover us with a golden cloud." And he brought down a cloud that dripped golden dew onto the grass. And there they lay down together and they wrapped their arms around each other, and they kissed. And Zeus, smiling, relaxed, fell asleep in her arms.

And, as soon as he was asleep, Hera laid him tenderly down onto the grass. She leapt to her feet; she drew the shimmering robe over her shoulders; she clasped it with the golden clasp

40 and, invisible, she made her way down from the mountain, straight to the Greek camp. Invisible, she moved through the Greek camp, until she found Patroclus. And she filled Patroclus with sudden courage.

Patroclus borrows Achilles' armour (⊕ 3:30)

Patroclus ran through the screams and smoke down to where the breakers crash and drag, down to Achilles' hut. He ran inside. There was Achilles strumming a harp, as though this day was like any other. Patroclus said, "Achilles, listen. The ships are burning. Agamemnon, Menelaus, Odysseus – all of them have been wounded. Prince Hector of Troy is unstoppable!

5   If you will not fight today, lend me your armour. Let me wear it. You know, the very sight of it will put the Trojans to flight."

And so Patroclus begged to bring about his own death.

Achilles smiled. He said, "Very well then. Wear my armour! Ride in my chariot! Lead my army! You can be Achilles today. Drive the Trojans out of the camp. But be careful. You know Apollo

10   loves this city. If you were to threaten it, he would punish you and his punishments are awful and swift."

And so, for the first time, Patroclus took Achilles' well-made greaves and strapped them onto his legs. He put on Achilles' golden breastplate, covered in shimmering, silver stars. He put on Achilles' helmet with its black, nodding horsehair plume, bristling with terror. And then he said,

15   "My friend, you have entrusted these precious things to me. I will give that thing that I value most to you for safekeeping, until I return."

And then Patroclus took from his finger the wonderful golden ring. The golden ring, carved in the shape of a curling arrow, whose sharp point touched its feathered tail. That ring, Achilles had given him years before. Patroclus took it off and gave it to Achilles. Achilles put it onto his

20   finger. Patroclus climbed into the car of Achilles' chariot, and he set forth.

And the Trojans, torching the Greek ships, suddenly saw Achilles. They saw Achilles in his golden armour. They saw Achilles with his matchless Myrmidons behind him, and they were terrified. They dropped the torches they were holding. They ran in all directions. No word of Hector's would rally them. They climbed over the shattered palisade. They escaped to save

25   their own skins.

Patroclus' success upsets Zeus (🕐 4:38)

Patroclus, dressed in Achilles' armour – Patroclus, dressed as Achilles - rode out against the Trojans then. Death rode a chariot that day and the Myrmidons fastened on the Trojans, as when a little boy hears a strange sound from within a dead, hollow tree and picks up a stick and pushes the stick into the shadows, and the wasps who have nested inside come pouring
5   out – a seething, black cloud of frenzied rage.

So the Myrmidons fell upon the Trojans. They tumbled to the ground with jolting groans, splintered teeth, shattered bones. Like a hawk swooping from the sky into starlings, Patroclus drove them out of the camp, across the blasted battlefield, until he saw the walls of Troy rising before him, until he saw Hector, man-killing Hector, Prince of Troy, fleeing before his charge.

10   Patroclus, mother's son, did you forget? Did the blur of battle, the clamour of kills, befuddle your mind? Or did you decide to try the last, despite Achilles' warning? You went too far.

On the rocky crag on Mount Ida, Zeus woke up. And he smiled and he stretched and he yawned, and then he looked down at the battlefield and he saw the Trojans in full retreat. He saw Patroclus in Achilles' armour, driving the Trojans before him. And, behind Patroclus, the
15   Myrmidons and behind the Myrmidons the whole Greek army, pouring across the battlefield.

And among the Greeks he saw his wife, Hera, and his daughter, Athene, invisible. screeching and screaming with delight, splattered with blood and gore. And Zeus began to tremble with fury. He lifted his hands to his mouth and he bellowed, "Hera!"

And Hera stopped and she turned and she stared. And she would have been destroyed. She
20   would have been annihilated by the fury of Zeus' gaze, had she not still been wearing that belt of love and desire, which softened Zeus' heart towards her.

He said, "Hera! Athene! Go to Mount Olympus now and send me Apollo!" And, scuttling up into the sky, shaking, quaking with fear, the two goddesses disappeared.

And it wasn't long before Apollo, golden Apollo, was standing in front of Zeus. And Zeus said,
25   "Apollo, go to Hector and help him all you can."

And Trojan-loving Apollo wasted no time. As swift as thought, he flew into the city, and there on the battlements was Hector. He was driving down the Greeks. He was in the thick of the battle. Three times the golden-armoured one had clambered up the city walls. Three times they had driven him down with spears. And, suddenly, as Hector was fighting, he heard a voice
30   beside himself.

"Tut, tut, tut, tut, tut." He turned and there was a warrior he'd never seen before. And the warrior said, "Hector, why do you stay inside the city walls? Why do you not go out and fight that golden-armoured one? Who knows, perhaps Apollo would help you?"

And suddenly the warrior vanished, and, where he'd been standing there was a golden light
35 hanging on the air. And Hector was filled with spirit and awe in the knowledge he'd been in the
presence of one of the mighty gods.

He ran down the stone steps. He leapt into the car of his chariot. His charioteer whipped the
horses to a gallop. The great bronze gates of the city were thrown open and Hector rode out of
Troy.

Hephaestus replaces Achilles' armour (⌚ 6:15)

Back in the Greek camp, Achilles was waiting for his friend Patroclus to return. He was pacing
back and forth. He heard a sound, a thousand Trojan voices crying out as one, crying out with
joy. And then a strange thing. His hand, Achilles' hand was wet and sticky. He lifted it to his
face. The ring, the golden ring of Aphrodite, the golden ring carved in the shape of a curling
5   arrow whose sharp point touched its feathered tail, the golden ring Patroclus had entrusted to
Achilles for safe keeping – that ring was bleeding. Blood was weeping from it down his finger,
down the back of his hand, down the back of his arm, dropping from his elbow into the mud.
And he knew, Achilles knew, what had happened.

King Odysseus made his way from the battlefield, knowing he'd have to break the awful news
10   to Achilles of Patroclus' death. He made his way through the camp, down to where the
breakers suck and drag. He opened the door of Achilles' hut and he saw he was too late.

Achilles was naked on all fours, convulsing. His skin smeared with filth and ash, streaked with
his own tears. In his fists, clumps of his own hair that he had torn from his head. His eyes,
bulging red and bloodshot. He was grinding together his teeth with an awful guttural sound.
15   And then he threw back his head and he loosed such a scream of fury and sorrow Odysseus
ran from the hut. He could not bear to see such sights. He could not bear to hear such sounds.

Thetis heard the scream. She came at once. She stood over her son. "Mother, my best friend,
Patroclus, has been taken from me. Hector killed him and he stripped my burnished armour
from his back! Before I die, I'll see that Hector crawling, coughing up his own bubbling blood! I
20   will fight him naked if need be!"

"My son," she said, "I will win you armour. Promise me you'll not go into battle until I return."
And she was gone into the heavens.

She rose up and up through the clouds, high and high, until she came to the slopes of Mount
Olympus. And she made her way across the mountain until she came to the palace of
25   Hephaestus, the crippled god of metalwork. And she made her way into his workshop. And
there he was, fashioning a golden tripod.

And when he saw Thetis, he got up to his feet, and he pulled the nose of the bellows out of the
embers, and he washed his hands on a dripping sponge. He said, "Thetis, Thetis, what brings
you here?"

30   And Thetis said, "Patroclus, Patroclus has been killed and my son Achilles' armour has been torn from his back. Man-slaying Hector has stolen Achilles' armour. And now my son has nothing to wear. Hephaestus, I beg you please, make him a new suit of armour."

And Hephaestus said, "I wish I could make him a suit of armour that would protect him from his fate, but I can make him a suit of armour that will fill his heart with joy, and will fill the eyes of all

35   men and women with wonder."

And Hephaestus put gold and silver and tin and bronze into melting vats, and he began to shape a suit of armour. And such a suit of armour it was: beautiful greaves of pliant tin; a breastplate of bronze that shone like the sun itself; a golden helmet with golden plume and golden tassels. And then he fashioned a shield, a magnificent shield. And on that shield he

40   wrought the earth and the sky, with all the stars, all the constellations. And the earth as two countries: one at peace, with a wedding dance and purple clusters of grapes and a trickling stream and grazing cattle; and the other country at war, with a city under siege and all the terrible tumult of the battlefield.

And, when the precious pieces were ready, Hephaestus gave them to Thetis and she seized

45   them in her hands and she thanked him with all of her heart. And then she descended down and down from the heavens to the earth.

Achilles' new armour (p. 105)

EPISODE 9 – The Anger of Achilles

Achilles goes in search of Hector (🕐 5:33)

When the dead body of Patroclus was brought from the battlefield, Achilles, murmuring to himself, pushed back the hair from the brow. He took a sponge and washed off all the blood and grime, and then he laid the body on a fur and all night he sat beside it, weeping.

Next morning his mother came with glorious armour. She laid it before him, piece by piece. It
5 was so bright his servants could not look at it. Achilles stood. He strapped on the greaves of pliant tin. He put on the breastplate. He put on the golden helmet with golden tassels and a golden plume. Each piece was shaped to perfection, cool against his skin. He felt lighter with them on, as though he wore invisible wings.

He picked up that wonderful shield that lit up the sky like the moon. He took a sword. He
10 stepped into the car of his chariot and there, in front of him, the four immortal horses – Lightfoot, Beauty, Dapple and Dancer. And he said, "This time bring your master home!"

"Yes," said Beauty. "We'll save your life today. But not for any want of speed or care did Hector strip Patroclus' back. It was a god. It was a god who killed him and the mighty gods will kill you too."

15 "What would you have me do?" Achilles said. "Cower in my hut while Hector struts in my father's armour? If I am meant to die here, far from my father and far from my mother, then so be it. But, before I die, I'll see the Trojans have their glut of bloody war!"

And he was out of the camp then, among his enemies then, like inhuman fire raging in the mountains, like a mountain lion, like the god of battle, until the ground was sticky with black
20 blood. Eyes blazing, teeth bared, heart pounding, scorning fear, the headlong runner, too bright to look at, ablaze with fury, cutting a path through flesh towards the city.

And all the Trojan warriors had fled through the city gates. The great bronze Scaean gates had been closed behind them. All the Trojan warriors had returned to the city, except for one. Hector stood outside, dressed in Achilles' armour, the golden breastplate emblazoned with
25 silver stars. He was looking this way and that way, watching and waiting.

And high overhead, his father, old Priam, the white-bearded father of Troy, leaned over the parapet of the city walls. He said, "Hector, my son, come inside! Or have the mighty gods condemned me to loiter on the outermost rim of old age, suffering intolerable grief?"

And Hector's mother, Hecuba, beckoned to him. And his wife, Andromache, with little Astyanax
30 in her arms, beckoned to him. But Hector turned his back on them all and he stood resolutely outside, compassing in all directions with his eyes.

And then he saw what he was looking for. Among the bronze helmets, with their horsehair plumes, he saw the golden helmet with golden plume and golden tassels. Achilles! And in that moment Achilles saw Hector. He leapt from his chariot. He ran across the battlefield, leaping
35 over shattered chariots, over disembowelled horses.

And, as he drew closer, Hector could see that his armour was dripping with blood and gore. And, as he drew closer still, Hector could see that his mouth was open and from his throat came a terrible screaming, screeching, keening cry of grief and fury.

And Hector looked down at the earth between his feet. He looked up at his father and his

40 mother and his son and his wife. And, in that moment, he knew that he wanted life more than any glorious death on the battlefield, and he turned and he ran. He knew every hill and hollow of the land. He knew every contour. He turned and he ran like a deer. But Achilles was after him, tracking him like a dog, following every twist and turn. Three times Hector ran round the city walls of Troy, with Achilles close behind him.

Hector's fate in the balance (⏱ 3:15)

And up on the rocky crag, on Mount Ida, Zeus lifted the golden scales and into one pan of the scales he put the luck of Hector. And into the other pan of the scales he put the luck of Achilles. And then he watched as the luck of Hector sank down and down and down towards Hades' halls and the luck of Achilles soared up into the skies.

5 And in that moment all the gods and the goddesses deserted Hector. And in that moment Athene, owl-eyed Athene, invisible, swooped down out of the sky and stood outside the city walls in the shape of Deiphobus, Hector's brother, Deiphobus.

And, as Hector was running round the city walls, Deiphobus said, "Hector! Hector!"

And Hector turned and said, "Deiphobus, my brother, you alone have ventured through the city

10 gates and I love you for it."

And Deiphobus said, "Hector, why don't we make a stand against Achilles, you and I together?"

And Hector nodded and he turned and he faced Achilles. And Achilles curled his lips back from his teeth and he screamed and, with all the strength of his arm, he hurled a spear at Hector.

15 But Hector dodged to one side and the spear lodged quivering in the ground behind him. And Hector lifted his own spear. And in that moment he didn't see his brother Deiphobus vanish. He didn't see Athene, invisible, pulling his spear out of the ground and carrying it through the air. Hector threw his spear at Achilles and it struck Achilles' shield. It glanced to one side. And Hector turned. He said, "Deiphobus, my brother, give me Achilles' spear!"

20 But Deiphobus was gone. And he saw in that moment that Achilles was holding his own spear once again, and he knew that the mighty gods and goddesses had deserted him.

He drew his sword. He raised it above his shoulder. He ran towards Achilles. He could see his own reflection in Achilles' breastplate. Behind himself he could see the reflection of the city walls of Troy.

25 But already that spear, that spear that could cut through the wind itself, was singing through the air. It struck Hector in the throat. It jutted through the nape of his neck. He dropped to his knees. The red blood was frothing and bubbling in his mouth. He looked up and Achilles was

standing over him. He said, "Please, I beg you, do not let the Greek dogs tear my flesh by your hollow ships. Return my body to my own people."

30   But Achilles spat in his face. "You killed Patroclus. I won't drive the dogs from your flesh, not for any ransom!" And he put his foot onto Hector's face and he tore out the dripping, barbed spear. And Hector stretched his hands out to the earth and darkness descended on his eyes.

Achilles lays Patroclus to rest (🕐 4:16)

And Achilles dragged the body of Hector to his chariot. He tore off his armour. He threw it into the car of the chariot. And then, from his belt, he took a knife. He lifted one of Hector's feet and he pierced a hole through the heel, between the tendon and the bone, and the same with the other foot. And then he got a length of ox hide thong and he threaded it through the holes and

5   he tied it. And he tied the other end of the thong to the back of his chariot.

He leapt into the car of the chariot. He whipped the horses to a gallop and he drove them round and round the city walls of Troy – three times round, screaming and screaming.

And behind the chariot, the body of Hector bouncing, the face of Hector, tearing a furrow into the nourishing earth. And then Achilles drove his chariot across the plain, through the gates of

10   the palisade, and he was gone.

And the people of Troy, standing on the walls, on the turrets and the towers, they stood and they stared, appalled, mesmerised. And it was only when Achilles was out of sight that their tears came and they gave themselves over to dark despair.

When Achilles and his men returned to the Greek camp, they set to work. No time for rest!

15   Bone weary from battle, still in armour, they cut down trees. They built a pyre, a hundred feet in width and length. On top of the heap they put Patroclus. They killed dogs, horses, mules, goats. They surrounded the corpse with the dead.

They poured on oil and wine and honey, and then they set it aflame and, as the flames rose up, Achilles said, "Brothers, Patroclus goes across the river. Soon I will join him, the gods

20   decree. Swear to me that, when I die, you'll burn me too. You'll mingle my ashes with those of Patroclus so we will be together for all time." And his tears spattered onto his bloodstained armour.

Then he and his men rode their chariots around the flaming pyre. Then he and his men had a great feast. They ate and drank and sang in honour of their friend. And all through this

25   celebration, this mourning of the passing of their friend, Achilles would turn and run into the shadows and kick the battered corpse of Hector, stamp upon his limbs, spit into his face as the dogs gnawed at his flesh.

The corpses of two young men, Hector and Patroclus, both killed in battle: they were so alike in death that one could have been mistaken for the other.

EPISODE 10 – The Pity of Achilles

CD 3 tracks 1-2
total running time: 13:23

A father begs for the return of his son (⏱ 6:24)

Imagine old Priam, the white-bearded Priam of Troy. Imagine Priam, King of Troy, sitting on his golden throne like a statue. For two days he had not eaten. He had not drunk. He had not spoken. The only movement was the movement of tears, trickling down his cheeks and his beard and his neck.

5   And then at last he opened his mouth and he said, "Achilles cannot be altogether a godless man. And surely he loves his own father, old Peleus? I will go to him myself and I will beg him to return the body of our son, Hector. I will beg him, in the name of his father, to return the body of our son. And I will offer him Hector's weight in sparkling, yellow gold."

And Queen Hecuba buried her face in her hands and she said, "The old man has gone mad!
10   The mighty gods have addled his wits. That savage beast, that wild animal, will tear him limb from limb, just as he has destroyed our own son!"

But Priam took no notice of her. He got up to his feet. He made his way to the treasure house of the palace. He lifted the lids of chests and coffers and he took out gold: arm rings, radiant; shields, shining; burnished battle vests; decorated drinking vessels; golden goblets. He piled
15   gold upon gold upon gold.

And Paris followed him and Paris said, "Father, you cannot go to the Greek camp alone. At least take me with you!"

And Priam said, "No, I go alone."

"Then take somebody with you!"

20   And Priam said, "Very well. I will take little Polyxena with me." Now Polyxena was the youngest of all the children of Priam and Hecuba, a beautiful young woman.

And so it was that night a cart was harnessed to two horses and the cart was filled with gold. And Priam and Polyxena, with black cloaks over their shoulders and black hoods drawn down over their faces, climbed up onto the seat of the cart. And they shook the reins and the great
25   bronze gates of the city were opened and they made their way across the plain towards the Greek camp.

There was a full moon shining in the sky and, as they journeyed across the plain, they passed churned earth and splintered trees and shattered chariots and dead horses, swollen with decay, their hooves pointing up towards the stars. They passed the bodies of foot soldiers,
30   some still sticky with gore and some no more than tatters of skin clinging to bleached bones. And everywhere the scuttling of rats and the fighting of dogs over carrion. And everything black and grey and silver in the moonlight.

And, when they reached the gates of the palisade, some god must have been watching over them because the gates were open and the sentinels were asleep. And they made their way

35 across the Greek camp, the great curled prows of the ships dark against the silver sky above their heads. And at last they came to the seashore, where the waves suck and drag.

And there was the hut of Achilles. And old Priam clambered down from the seat of the cart and Polyxena stayed with the gold. But the old king made his way across and he lifted the latch of the door and he pushed it open. And there was Achilles, sitting alone, staring at the ground.

40 And old Priam ran across. He threw himself down at Achilles' feet. He curled his left arm over Achilles' knees. He kissed the man-slaying hands that had so recently been the death of his own son.

And he said, "It is a father's joy to hear his son returning home, to hear the sound of the doors swinging open and then the stamping of earth from sandals. And then perhaps he hears the

45 sound of a satchel or a shield being thrown onto the ground. And then he hears maybe a snatch of song, and he sees his own son come striding into his hall and pouring himself a cup of wine and drinking and wiping the froth from his lips. Achilles, even now as I am speaking, your father, old Peleus, will be dreaming of your return. He will be longing for your return, a return that I will never see. At least give me the body of Hector. I will pay for it with his weight

50 in sparkling, yellow gold."

Achilles relents – at a price (⏱ 6:59)

And it seemed to Achilles that he saw his own father before him. For years he'd cursed this Priam as the bullish father of a brutal brood. But now he saw white hair, white beard – an old man, scarred with care, trembling hand – a father who'd lost a son. And Achilles' eyes filled with tears. He put his hands on the old man's shoulders and the two men wept together as

5 though they were family, as though their sorrows were the same.

When his tears could no more come, Achilles said, "How much you've suffered! Such pain would crush my spirit. And you must have a heart of iron to walk among your mortal foes. How blessed we seemed when we were born, I and your son, Hector, both of us born the sons of kings. But both of us had been cursed by the gods. For my father too will soon discover he has

10 outlived his son. I grant your wish. You'll have his body and more. For however long you need to grieve him, to mourn his passing with proper honours, I'll hold back the Greek armies. I'll wait, I'll watch for grieving smoke."

And Achilles ordered that a weighing scales, an enormous weighing scales, be built outside his hut, each pan large enough to take the body of a grown man. And then, wrapped in a woollen

15 shroud, the corpse of Hector was laid at their feet.

And old Priam dropped to his knees and he began to fold back the layers of wool. And, as he did so, golden Apollo took pity on him and, with one movement of his hands, he undid all the damage that had been done, so that, when Priam folded back the last layer of wool, there was Hector's face in all of its beauty, as though he was asleep. And the old king kissed his son. He

20 kissed the forehead and the cheeks, and his tears splashed down onto Hector's face.

And then the body was lifted and it was laid onto one of the pans of the scales. And Polyxena began to unload gold from the cart. She piled gold upon gold upon gold upon gold. But, when the cart was empty, the body of Hector was still heavier. And so she unclasped the necklace from her throat and she threw it into the pan. She pulled bracelets and bangles from her wrists

25   and she threw them onto the pan. She pulled the rings from her fingers. And Achilles sat and he watched her, and as he watched her he fell in love with Polyxena.

And the last ring that she pulled from her finger and threw into the pan lifted the body of Hector. The scales balanced perfectly. And the body was taken and it was laid tenderly in the cart.

30   And Achilles said, "Old man! Princess! Come and eat with me before you go!"

And so it was that old Priam and Polyxena sat down at a table with Achilles. And meat and bread and wine were served. And Achilles broke the white bread with his own hands and he offered it to them.

And, when they had finished eating, Achilles reached across and he took Priam's hand and he

35   kissed it. And he said, "Old man, we mortals are wretched things and the gods who know no care have woven sorrow into the pattern of our lives."

And then he reached across and he took Polyxena's hand and he kissed it. And, as he kissed it, he pressed onto her finger that ring, that golden ring in the shape of a curved arrow whose sharp tip touches its feathered tail. And Polyxena looked at the ring. And then she and her

40   father got up to their feet and they climbed onto the seat of the cart and they shook the reins and they made their way across the plain and back to the city of Troy.

And for ten days there were funeral games in honour of Hector. And then, on the eleventh day, a pyre was built outside the city walls and the body of Hector was laid on the pyre. And all that day the heat of the fire's heart consumed the house of bone.

45   And, when all had been reduced to white ash, Paris gathered the charred bones of his brother and he wrapped them in a crimson cloth and they were put into a golden casket. And earth was piled over the casket and stones over the earth and earth over the stones. And then the people of Troy returned to the city, all but Andromache. She knelt beside her husband's grave and she said, "Sweet Hector, I could not even hold your hand when you died."

EPISODE 11 – Love and Death

Achilles' secret is revealed (⏱ 6:12)

The day after Hector's funeral the awful tumult resumed. And, out on the battlefield, Achilles was in the thick of the battle, severing heads with every stroke of his sword. That night he was back on the battlefield, wrapped in a black cloak, clambering over the corpses, making his way so that he could look up at the tops of the walls of Troy, scanning them, desperate for a

5   glimpse of that pretty Trojan princess, Polyxena.

Day after day he fought. Night after night he skulked, until eventually, exasperated, he bribed a Trojan foot soldier to take a note to her, begging her to meet him outside the walls in an ancient grove of olive trees.

And Polyxena read that letter and she remembered Achilles, she remembered his beauty. She

10 looked at the golden ring on her finger and she was filled with love and longing for him. And that night, when the sky was bright with stars, she wrapped the black cloak over her shoulders and she hurried through the streets of Troy and through a secret gate, and across the plain to the olive grove.

Some of the trees were still standing and some were splintered, lying on the ground. And as

15 she drew close, Achilles stepped out of the shadows and she ran into his arms. And those hands that had so recently been the death of her brother, fondled her tenderly. And they lay down on the grass together, locked in one another's arms.

But nothing is hidden from the mighty gods and goddesses. And high overhead Aphrodite, the goddess of love, called to golden Apollo and she said, "Apollo, look at this! Look at this! Look

20 what I've made happen!"

And Apollo looked down and he said, "Shameless Polyxena! Shameless, shameless Aphrodite!"

And Aphrodite said, "But Apollo, don't you understand? This is our chance. Go to Paris. Tell him that his sister, Polyxena, has taken a lover, a Greek lover. Tell him to follow her tomorrow

25 night, with a bow and a quiver full of arrows, and I'll put what words I can into Polyxena's mouth."

And suddenly Apollo understood. And he threw back his head and he shouted with laughter. And, as swift as thought, he flew through the air into Troy, into the palace of Paris, into the bedchamber, where Paris was lying asleep in Helen's arms.

30 And golden Apollo entered Paris' dreams. "Paris, did you know that your sister, Polyxena, has taken a lover, a Greek lover. Follow her tomorrow night with a bow and a quiver full of arrows."

And in that moment Paris woke up, with the words echoing in his mind. And all the next day he watched his sister, Polyxena, but she gave no clue, no hint, no indication, until the night came and the sky brightened with stars and he saw her hurrying through the streets in a black cloak

35 and through a secret gate. And he grabbed a bow and a quiver full of arrows. And he followed

her. He followed her across the plain. He saw the grove of olive trees. He saw a figure stepping out of the shadows. He saw Polyxena running into his arms. And then Paris felt a cold shudder from the nape of the neck to the root of the spine. Achilles! He flattened himself against the ground. He pressed his face into the dirt, hardly daring to breath.

40 And, as he lay there, he could hear the lovers talking and laughing. And then he heard the sound of them lying down together. And Paris lifted his head. He peered over the trunk of a fallen tree. He could see Achilles. He could see the back of his head, his shoulders, the small of his back, the backs of his legs, his heels.

And then he heard Polyxena say, "My lover, I don't understand. You have been fighting in this
45 war for as long as I can remember, since I was five years old. And yet you're unscratched. There's no mark, no bruise, no scar on your body. Why?"

And Achilles said, "Polyxena, when I was a baby my mother, Thetis, carried me down to the dark waters of the river Styx. She lowered me into the river. Wherever the water touched I am invulnerable. I cannot be harmed. The only place I can be harmed is where she held me, my
50 heel."

Paris drew an arrow from the quiver. He fitted the arrow to the bowstring. He drew the bowstring back. He loosed the arrow. And it would have gone wide, wide of its mark, if golden Apollo had not been watching and waiting. He seized it as it flew through the air. He ran across and he plunged the point of it into Achilles' heel. And a great shudder went through Achilles' body and the life went out of him in one breath.

55 And Paris leapt to his feet. "Achilles is dead! Achilles is dead!"

He ran back to the city. He ran from street to street. "Achilles is dead! Achilles is dead!" In every house lanterns were lit, doors were thrown open, people came running into the streets. "Achilles is dead! Achilles is dead!"

A mother honours her famous son (⏱ 5:59)

Back in the Greek camp, King Odysseus was woken by a great commotion. He searched for the source of the sound. He found himself before Achilles' stables. He opened up the doors. There were the wonderful white horses, rearing up in the air, kicking the air with their front legs, kicking at their stalls with their back legs, rolling their great eyes, snorting.

5 Odysseus harnessed them to a chariot. They took him out of the camp, out across the blasted battlefield, until he was near the walls of Troy – to an ancient olive grove. Odysseus climbed down. He made his way from behind one tree to the next until he found a girl, a Trojan girl, kneeling in the grass, weeping, her shoulders shaking. And, in front of her, lying, stretched out, lifeless – the body of Achilles! Achilles was dead!

10 He pushed her away. He gathered up the body back into the chariot and back to the Greek camp.

"Achilles is dead! Achilles is dead!" The great bronze Scaean gates of the city were thrown open and the people followed Paris across the plain to the olive grove. But there was no sign of Achilles. There was only Polyxena, sobbing and sobbing and sobbing and looking at the ring

15   on her finger as it dribbled blood down the back of her hand, down her arm and the blood was dripping from her elbow onto the earth.

By the time King Odysseus returned to the Greek camp, everyone was awake. They followed him with flaming torches from the gates to the gathering place. He lifted the slight body of Achilles out of the chariot and laid it in the mud and the men around him gasped.

20   He looked serene in death. All through his life Achilles' face had been twisted with passion, with worry and care. But now all those passions were gone. It was as though he was asleep.

As they feasted on his beauty, his mother came from the sea, her face shrouded in a veil. She scooped up the body of her son and, as though he was still alive, as though he was a little boy who could not sleep, she rocked him. She sang to him.

25   The men went back to their huts. They left mother and son alone together. She burned his body.

And, as Thetis watched the flames rise up, she thought of her wedding day, the happiest day of her life. How full of hope she'd been! She thought of all the wonderful wedding gifts: the spear, the golden breastplate, the wonderful ring, the four white horses, the ant warriors… and

30   then she remembered the last gift. And she walked to Achilles' hut and there inside in the corner, squatting, gathering shadows, there it was, the gift of the god of the dead. A black urn. Inlaid in silver across its front, a picture, an image of three goddesses, the three Fates. The first who spins out the thread of a life, the second who measures out the life's length and the third who cuts it.

35   She picked up the urn. She found the ashes of Patroclus and put them in. She went outside. Now the pyre was only glowing ashes, shining bones. She put those ashes and bones into the urn and mingled them with those of Patroclus. Then she walked out of the camp. She carried the urn, the ashes, out of the sight, out of the reach of any mortal man.

She buried it on a headland that overlooks the sea. And, when she had finished, she said, "My

40   dear child, not for you the stretching shadow, not for you the ripening grape, not for you the joy of children. You chose glory."

Odysseus' big idea (🕑 4:29)

Next day, no sign of mother or son in the Greek camp. King Odysseus called a meeting in the gathering place. He said, "He is dead. If he, Achilles, could not breach these walls, if the greatest warrior in the greatest army in the history of the world could not break down these walls, then force of arms never will!

5   "I have a plan. Years ago, when we Greek kings first heard of Helen's beauty, we gathered in the palace of her foster father in the hope that we could win her hand. He slaughtered a stallion before us, laid out the severed pieces across the floor and made each of us stand upon a piece of that stallion and swear that, when Helen made her choice, we would accept it. And, if ever she was stolen from her husband, we would come to his aid. And so this business

10   will end just the way it began."

The next morning, Odysseus' men set to work. They cut down trees and, with the wood of those trees, they carved. They carved great legs, great flanks, a long neck, a mane, a long head, a tail. They set it on a huge platform. Then Odysseus and six of the bravest of his men climbed into the belly of it and a secret trap door was closed behind them. The whole thing

15   was painted black. Golden words painted along the side. Then the men outside burned the whole camp, the palisade, the huts. Then they dragged their ships down to the sea and sailed out of sight of the city of Troy.

The next morning, as the dawn took her golden throne, the people of Troy, from the walls, from the turrets, from the towers, they saw that the Greeks were gone. The Greek ships had

20   disappeared. Where the camp had been there was smoke rising up into the blue sky. They looked at one another. They said "Achilles is dead and now the Greeks have gone! The Greeks have gone home! The war is over!"

They rubbed their eyes. They looked again. And, in the smoke, there was something else dark against the blue waves of the sea. It was a horse, an enormous horse. The great bronze

25   Scaean gates were thrown open. The people of Troy poured across the plain to the seashore. They made their way between the burning fires and there was the great horse, stretching high above them. They walked around it, staring at it, amazed. There were letters written in gold, 'a gift for the goddess Athene'.

And the priests and the wise men, they looked at one another and they said, "We must take

30   the horse into the city. We must set it in front of the temple to Athene, the goddess of war and wisdom, and then we will have a celebration. The war is over at last!"

And the people of Troy lifted the great platform up onto their shoulders. They carried the horse across the plain, through the gates, into the city. They set it outside the great temple of Athene. And then trestle tables were loaded with food and the people of Troy sat down and they ate

35   and they drank and they drank and they ate, until their bellies were hanging over their belts,

until their heads were swimming with wine. And then they went to their beds and they lay down and they fell into the sweet, oblivious balm of sleep.

A couple reunited (⊕ 4:34)

When even the dogs were asleep, the belly of the wooden horse swung open and down tumbled a rope ladder. And down that ladder climbed Odysseus and his six men. And they crept from shadow to shadow to the bronze Scaean gates. They slit the throats of the guards who slept there and then they opened up the gates of Troy from the inside.

5   Meanwhile the rest of the Greek fleet had sailed back from where they'd been hiding. They sailed back under cover of darkness. And the ships, they reached the beach, and the armies poured forth over the battlefield and into Troy. And, every time they found a house, they put it to the torch.

And, running through the burning street Menelaus, red-haired Menelaus, king of Sparta,
10   running this way and that way, until he found the palace of Paris. He threw open the doors; he cut the throats of the servants who tried to block his way; he ran up the stairs, pushed open the door of the bedchamber.

And there was Paris, lying asleep in Helen's arms. Menelaus lifted his spear above his shoulder and, with all the strength of both arms, he brought the point of it down. And the blood
15   spread out across the sheet. And high overhead, Aphrodite, the goddess of love, was watching. And, as she saw Paris die, she remembered that beautiful youth, that beautiful young man on the slopes of Mount Ida, all those years before. She remembered beautiful Paris choosing her.

And high overhead, Hera, queen of heaven, Athene, the goddess of war and wisdom, looked
20   down at the blood welling out over the sheets. And they remembered the moment that Paris had chosen Aphrodite over them. And Aphrodite looked down and she saw Helen. She saw Helen waking up and she took pity on her. And, with one gesture of her hand, she drew the arrow, the invisible arrow, from Helen's heart, as though she was pulling the thorn out of a foot. Helen awoke then, as though from some dream. She slid her hand across the bed. Blood! The
25   blood of Paris! Paris was dead!

She felt nothing. She looked up. There was her husband, red-haired Menelaus, his face a mask of hate. She stood up. She stretched out her hands towards him and, as he looked into her face for the first time in ten years, all his hatred, all his resentment melted into love and longing for her. And they fell into each other's arms and the beauty returned to Menelaus' skin.

30   And Agamemnon, the high king of all the Greeks, ran through the blazing city, until he came to the palace of Priam. He ran up the stairs, he pushed open the door of the bedchamber. And there was the old king, the white-bearded father of Troy, lying asleep on his bed. Agamemnon seized the head in his arm, as though he was holding a sheaf of wheat. And he drew his sword

across the throat, as though he was cutting through dry stalks of corn. And he threw the blood-

35 dripping head down onto the floor.

And, from high high overhead, golden Apollo looked down at the dead king and he remembered the founding of the city of Troy, the city that he loved the best of all. And he remembered the gifts and the offerings that old Priam had made to him.

Outside Odysseus was running back and forth through the streets, shouting at his men. They

40 had gone mad. They had gone wild with the desire for revenge. Odysseus shouted at them as they dragged Hector's wife, Andromache, up onto the walls of Troy, as they wrenched from her grasp her baby boy, and threw the baby from the walls of the city into the darkness and down onto the rocks below.

The gods have the last word (🕒 4:48)

And from high overhead, great Zeus, the cloud-compeller, looked down, he looked down at the shattered baby on the rocks. And he remembered Astyanax in Hector's arms; he remembered the baby weeping and laughing. And, if I could sing, I would sing of the mighty gods and goddesses standing, staring, looking down at the city as it burned. And those gods and

5 goddesses, who had enjoyed every twist and turn of the battlefield, stared now, appalled. And they began to tremble with fury!

Zeus, father of the gods, loosed a sheaf of thunderbolts. Each one struck a turret or a tower, and the turrets and the towers came toppling down onto the Greeks. The god of the sea, Poseidon, clapped his hands. There was an earthquake then. Great cracks appeared in the

10 city streets. The city began to collapse in on itself.

And through the blazing, crumbling city, Greek soldiers were dragging women as slaves. They were dragging them by their hair through the streets, slippery with blood. They were dragging Andromache, Polyxena. And old queen Hecuba was dragged through the great bronze Scaean gates. And, as the old queen was dragged through the gates, she turned and she saw

15 the city blazing, like a burning torch with red flames and yellow flames like flickering snakes, rising up into the sky. And, in that moment, she remembered her dream and she knew that her dream had come true.

If I could sing, I would sing of how the Greeks ran across the battlefield, cowering from the gods' fury. They clambered aboard their ships and they set off out across the boiling sea.

20 And the weeks passed and the months passed and the years passed. And, if I could sing, I would sing of the mighty gods looking down from the high slopes of Mount Olympus. And all they could see where the city had once stood was a pile of rubble, shattered marble, shattered granite, scorched timbers jutting out of stone. And down there, on the soft grass, they saw a horse's skull, bleached white by the sun, crawling with black ants. And at the edge of one of

25 the rivers there was a reed, and around the stem of the reed was a golden ring in the shape of an arrow, whose sharp point touched its feathered tail. And down here, by this mossy stone,

there was a golden helmet. And inside the golden helmet, a field mouse had made a soft nest of human hair.

And then Eris, the goddess of strife and arguing said, "Just think! All of this because of one golden apple!" And Aphrodite took the apple from her pocket, stared at it and said nothing.

30

The wooden horse (p. 115)

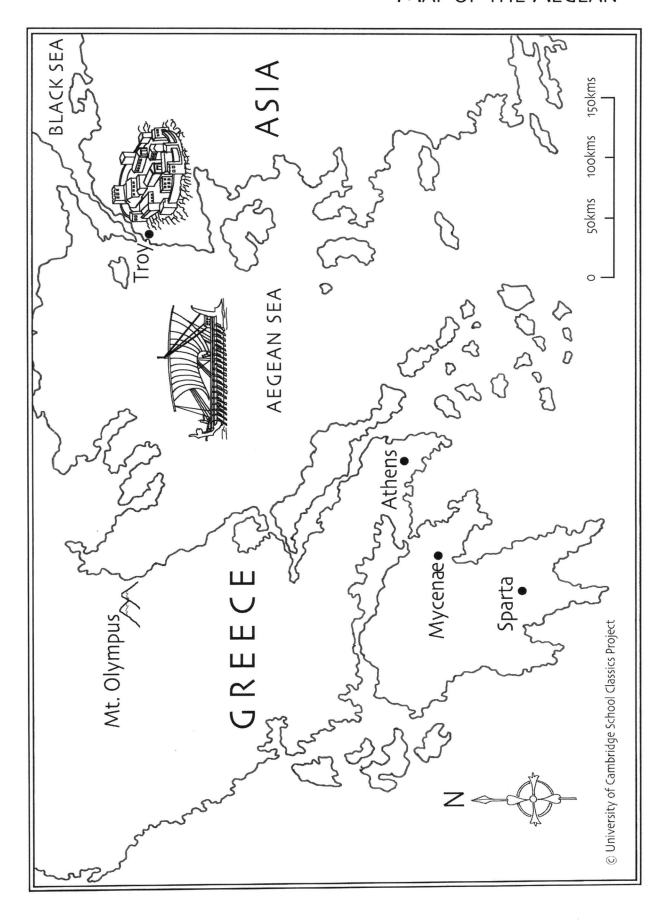

BLACK SEA

ASIA

Troy

AEGEAN SEA

Mt. Olympus

GREECE

Athens

Mycenae

Sparta

N

0   50kms   100kms   150kms

© University of Cambridge School Classics Project

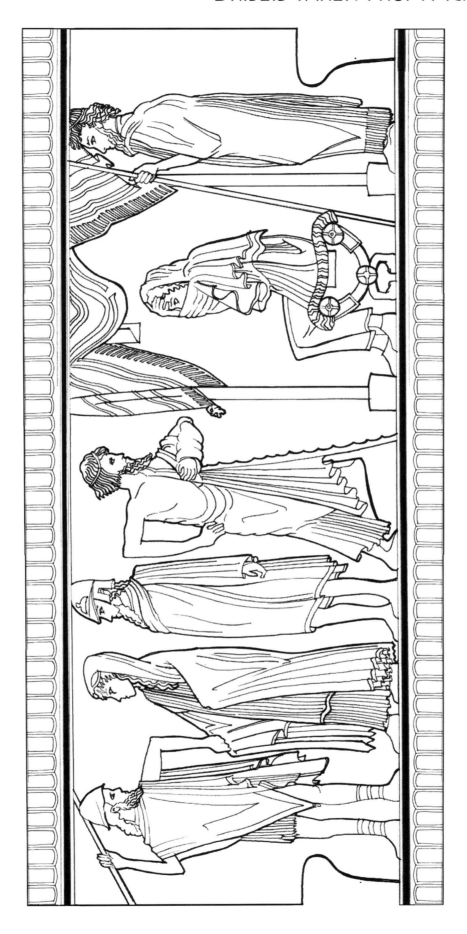

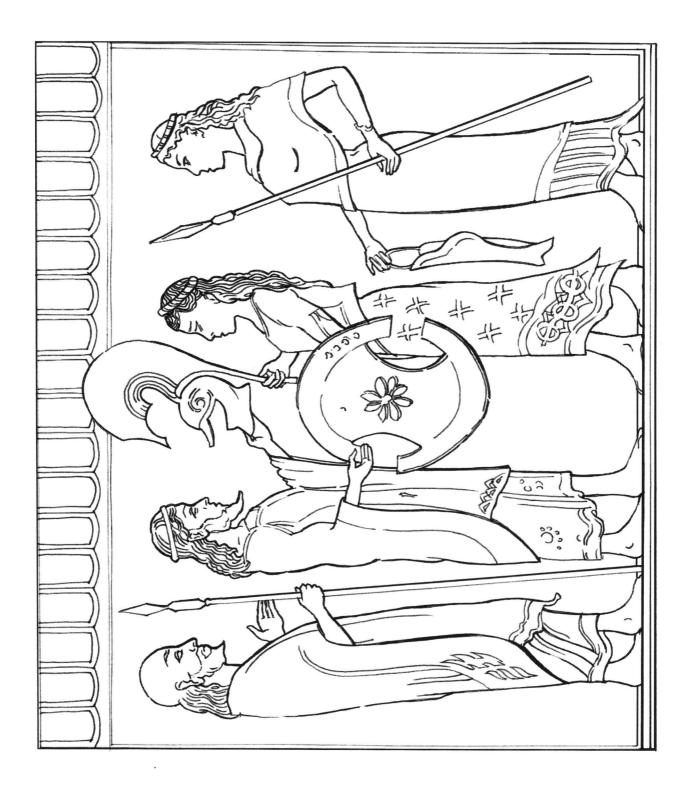

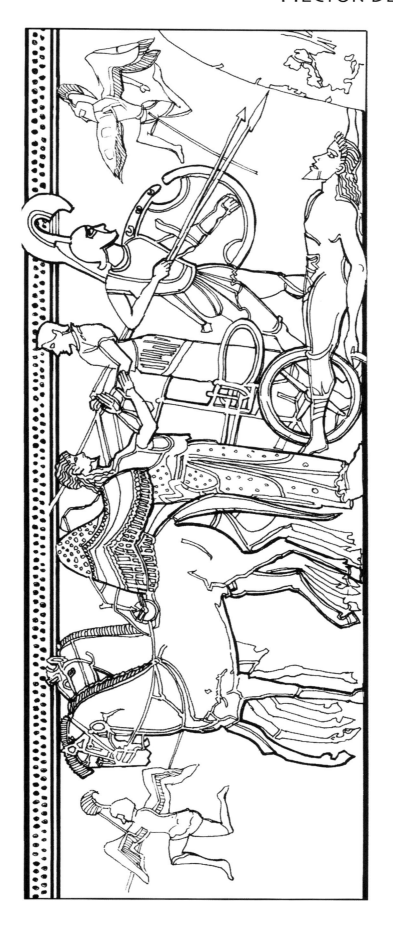

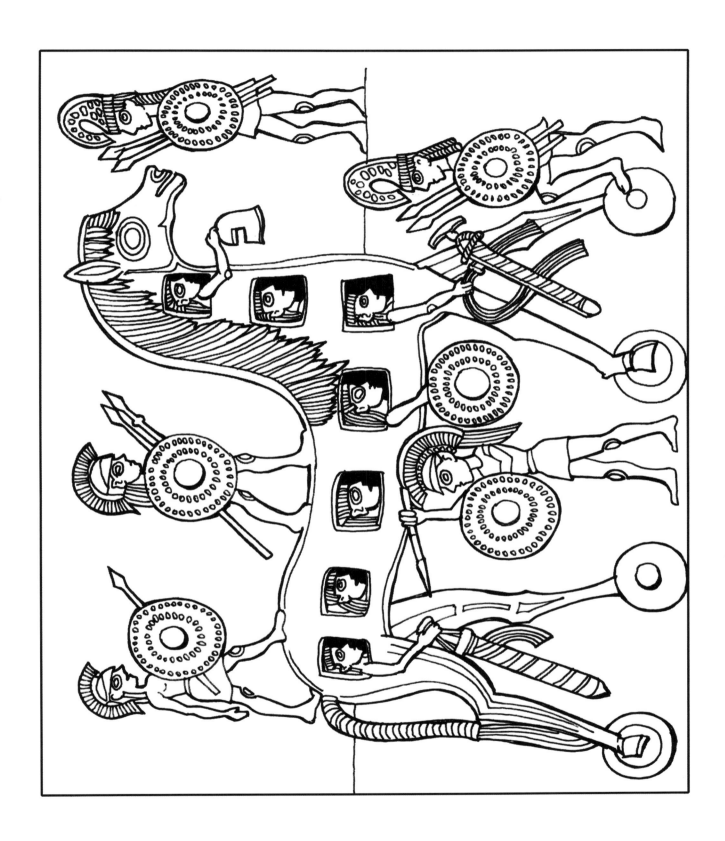

NOTES ON THE ILLUSTRATIONS

Peleus and Thetis (p. 87)
Based on a cup by Peithinos, c. 500 BC. Antikenmuseum, Berlin-Charlottenburg.
Peleus seems to kneel before Thetis rather than wrestle with her. He does not appear too troubled by the lion on his back or the snakes entwining themselves round his arm and leg. Though these animals represent the different shapes that Thetis adopted to avoid Peleus' grasp, Peleus' sword remains in its scabbard: he does not want to harm her.

Eris (p. 89)
Based on Little Master cup, c. 560 BC. Antikenmuseum, Berlin-Charlottenburg.
Eris, the goddess of arguing and trouble, is shown in the conventional pose of someone running at full speed. Is she always dashing about, causing mischief? She wears winged sandals, like Hermes (see p.81). Her name is written below in Greek script, filling out the circular space available to the artist.

The judgement of Paris (p. 91)
Based on a vase from Vulci, c. 520 BC. British Museum, London.
On the right we can see Paris, ready to choose the winner of the golden apple. He is holding a lyre (linking him perhaps to Apollo, god of music as well as archery, and the protector of Troy). On his left stands Hermes, the messenger of the gods, who can be recognised by his staff, traveller's hat and winged sandals. Hermes looks as though he is introducing to Paris the three goddesses on his left. Of the goddesses only Athene can be identified, by her snake-trimmed aegis (breastplate) and helmet; the other two are Hera and Athene.

Map of the Aegean (p.93)
Even this simplified map gives an impression of the number of islands scattered across the Aegean, many of which were visited by Paris and Helen as they made their leisurely way from Sparta to Troy.

On the walls of Troy (p. 95)
This artist's impression sketches the view from Troy across the plain on which so much of the fighting was to take place. In the distance we can see the shoreline of the Aegean sea and the Greek ships arriving from Sparta.

General battle scene (p. 97)
Based on a Chalcidian vase by the Inscription Painter, c. 540 BC. National Gallery of Victoria, Melbourne, Australia.
This confused scene is all limbs and weapons. In addition to the spears (which contribute so much to the composition) children will be able to pick out the plumed helmets, greaves (shin guards) and shields with prominent designs on the bosses. The shape of these shields here is more in keeping with the sixth century BC, when the vase was made, than the thirteenth century BC, when the Trojan War took place.

Menelaus and Paris (p. 99)
Based on an amphora by the Amasis Painter, c. 540 BC. Private collection.
In response to the challenge laid down by Paris, Menelaus (on the left) meets Paris in a duel. Each fighter is accompanied by an attendant. As is usually the case on Greek vases, the dominant figure occupies the left-hand position in the composition.

Briseis taken from Achilles (p. 101)
Based on a cup by the Briseis Painter, c. 480 BC. British Museum, London.
After his very public argument with Achilles, Agamemnon insisted on taking away Achilles' favourite slave, Briseis, as a way of asserting his authority as commander of the Greek armies. In this picture Briseis (second from the left) is being led away from Achilles' tent by two attendants, while Achilles (second from right) stays sitting on a stool, his face covered (perhaps to conceal his distress?).

Hector and Andromache (p. 103)

Based on a Chalcidian vase, 550-530 BC. Martin von Wagner Museum der Universität Würzburg.
On the original vase the names of all the figures are written beside them. From the left they are Helen, Paris, Andromache, Hector and Cebriones (Hector's attendant). Hector's stature as a fighter is emphasised by his helmet and prominent shield, and in contrast to Helen and Paris, Hector and Andromache look each other full in the face. Noticeably absent from this painting of the scene is the baby Astyanax, who burst into tears at the sight of his father's plumed helmet.

Achilles' new armour (p. 105)

Based on a black figure vase, sixth century BC. British Museum, London.
With the death of Patroclus Achilles loses his armour. Before he can go out to fight Hector, he has to have new armour made by Hephaestus, the god of metal-working. Here Zeus presents Achilles' new armour to Thetis, who had persuaded Hephaestus to undertake the task. Behind Thetis one of her sisters holds a spear and greaves. For obvious reasons the artist has not tried to show on the shield the very detailed scenes described in the second part of Episode 8 (closely based on Homer's description in the *Iliad*).

Achilles and Hector (p. 107)

Based on a vase by the Berlin Painter, 490-480 BC. British Museum, London.
This picture captures the moment when Hector is deserted by the gods. The figure on the right is Apollo, turning his back on Hector with a final look over his shoulder. Meanwhile Achilles, urged on by Athene (on the far left), presses home his advantage. The angle of the fighters' spears emphasises Achilles' forward movement and Hector's backward stumble.

Hector desecrated (p. 109)

Based on a vase by the Leagros Group, c. 510-500 BC. Delos Museum.
In this scene the painter has merged two elements of Homer's story, Achilles' lament at the tomb of Patroclus (shown as a mound on the extreme right) and his desecration of Hector's body which he attaches to his chariot and drags round the walls of Troy. Between Achilles and the tomb floats the winged soul of Patroclus (Hector's can be seen on the far left). At Achilles' feet lies the body of Hector, face up here rather than face down as in Homer's *Iliad*.

Priam and Achilles (p. 111)

Based on an amphora, c. 540 BC. Staatliche Kunstsammlungen, Kassel.
Priam stretches out his hands towards the body of Hector, who is lying as if asleep. Behind Priam stands Briseis with her veil pulled aside as a mark of respect. Achilles lies on a couch above Hector, his hand pointing downwards, perhaps to indicate that he is willing to return Hector's body to the Trojans for formal burial.

The death of Achilles (p. 113)

Based on red-figure vase by the Niobid Painter, c. 460 BC. Antikenmuseum, Ruhr-Universität, Bochum.
This rather crude depiction of the death of Achilles is slightly different from the description in Episode 11. Instead of being caught with Polyxena, Achilles is shown here in full armour, apparently about to fight Paris. But on one point the two versions agree: the death of Achilles is brought about by Apollo (centre) redirecting an arrow fired by Paris (left).

The wooden horse (p. 115)

Based on a clay relief storage vessel, c. 670-650 BC. Mykonos Museum.
With naïve simplicity the artist shows the wooden horse brimming with soldiers ready to spring out and slaughter the Trojans once the horse has been dragged inside the walls of Troy. The horse is already equipped with wheels to make the process easier.

CHARACTERS AND PLACES (in order of appearance)

Key: ⚔ Immortal   ♥ Mortal   ⛰ Place

	name	details	episode
⛰	Mt. Olympus	home of the gods	1
⚔	Zeus	king of the gods	1
⛰	Aegean Sea	sea between Greece and modern Turkey	1
⛰	Greece	country of the Mediterranean	1
⚔	Poseidon	god of the sea	1
⚔	Thetis	mother of Achilles	1
♥	Peleus	father of Achilles	1
⚔	Athene	goddess of wisdom and war	1
⚔	Ares	god of war	1
⚔	Aphrodite	goddess of love and beauty	1
♥	Myrmidons	race of warriors, once ants, under Achilles	1
⚔	Hades	god of the Dead; the Underworld	1
⚔	Fates	3 goddesses who decide the length of a life	1
⚔	Eris	goddess of arguing and trouble	1
⚔	Hera	queen of the gods	1
⛰	Styx	river of the Underworld	1
♥	Patroclus	Greek hero and friend of Achilles	1
♥	Achilles	greatest of the Greek heroes	1
⛰	Troy	city on coast of modern Turkey	2
♥	Priam	king of Troy	2
♥	Hecuba	queen of Troy	2
♥	Hector	prince of Troy; eldest son of Priam	2
♥	Deiphobus	prince of Troy; son of Priam	2
♥	Paris	prince of Troy; son of Priam; lover of Helen	2
⛰	Mt. Ida	mountain near Troy	2
⛰	Europe	a continent, part of the world where Greece was	2
⛰	Asia	a continent, part of the world where Troy was	2
⚔	Hermes	messenger of the gods	2
♥	Helen	queen of Sparta; wife of Menelaus; lover of Paris	2
♥	Menelaus	king of Sparta; husband of Helen	2
⛰	Sparta	city in Greece	2
⛰	Cranae	island where Paris & Helen spent their first night	3
♥	Agamemnon	most powerful king in Greece	3
♥	Calchas	Greek seer or prophet	3
⛰	Skyros	island where Achilles was hidden as a girl	3
♥	Odysseus	king of Ithaca, Greece	3
⛰	Scaean	one of the gates of Troy	3
♥	Cygnus	son of Poseidon; ally of the Trojans	4
	Beauty	horse of Achilles	4
⛰	Scamander	river near Troy	4
⛰	Xanthus	river near Troy	5
⚔	Apollo	god of light, archery and music; founder of Troy	5
♥	Pandarus	Trojan archer	5
♥	Briseis	slave girl taken from Achilles by Agamemnon	6
♥	Andromache	wife of Hector	7
♥	Astyanax	baby son of Hector	7
⛰	Black Sea	sea to the north of Greece and modern Turkey	7
⛰	Nile	main river in Egypt	7
⚔	Hephaestus	god of metal-working	8
♥	Polyxena	youngest daughter of Priam	10

CHARACTERS AND PLACES (listed alphabetically)

Key: ✍ Immortal   ♥ Mortal   🛏 Place

	name	details	further description
♥	Achilles	greatest of the Greek heroes	swift-runner
🛏	Aegean Sea	sea between Greece and modern Turkey	
♥	Agamemnon	most powerful king in Greece	high king
♥	Andromache	wife of Hector	
✍	Aphrodite	goddess of love and beauty	
✍	Apollo	god of light, archery and music; founder of Troy	golden; Trojan-loving
✍	Ares	god of war	red-eyed
🛏	Asia	a continent, part of the world where Troy was	
♥	Astyanax	baby son of Hector	
✍	Athene	goddess of wisdom and war owl-eyed	
	Beauty	horse of Achilles	
🛏	Black Sea	sea to the north of Greece and modern Turkey	
♥	Briseis	slave girl taken from Achilles by Agamemnon	
♥	Calchas	Greek seer or prophet far-sighted	
🛏	Cranae	island where Paris & Helen spent their first night	
♥	Cygnus	son of Poseidon; ally of the Trojans	white-haired; white-faced; white-eyed
♥	Deiphobus	prince of Troy; son of Priam	
✍	Eris	goddess of arguing and t rouble	
🛏	Europe	a continent, part of the world where Greece was	
✍	Fates	3 goddesses who decide the length of a life	
🛏	Greece	country of the Mediterranean	
✍	Hades	god of the Dead; the Underworld	lord of the realm of many guests
♥	Hector	prince of Troy; eldest son of Priam	
♥	Hecuba	queen of Troy	
♥	Helen	queen of Sparta; wife of Menelaus; lover of Paris	
✍	Hephaestus	god of metal-working	
✍	Hera	queen of the gods	queen of heaven; ox-eyed
✍	Hermes	messenger of the gods	
♥	Menelaus	king of Sparta; husband of Helen	red-haired
🛏	Mt. Ida	mountain near Troy	
🛏	Mt. Olympus	home of the gods	
♥	Myrmidons	race of warriors, once ants, under Achilles	
🛏	Nile	Main river in Egypt	
♥	Odysseus	King of Ithaca, Greece	cunning; clever; man of nimble wits
♥	Pandarus	Trojan archer	
♥	Paris	prince of Troy; son of Priam; lover of Helen	
♥	Patroclus	Greek hero and friend of Achilles	
♥	Peleus	father of Achilles	warlike
♥	Polyxena	youngest daughter of Priam	
✍	Poseidon	god of the sea	king of the tumbling foam
♥	Priam	king of Troy	golden-crowned; white-bearded
🛏	Scaean	one of the gates of Troy	
🛏	Scamander	river near Troy	
🛏	Skyros	island where Achilles was hidden as a girl	
🛏	Sparta	city in Greece	
🛏	Styx	river of the Underworld	
✍	Thetis	mother of Achilles	sea-nymph
🛏	Troy	city on coast of modern Turkey	
🛏	Xanthus	river near Troy	
✍	Zeus	king of the gods	great father; father-god; cloud-compeller